VOLUNTEERING
AROUND THE GLOBE

VOLUNTEERING
AROUND THE GLOBE

Life-Changing Travel Adventures

SUZANNE STONE

Capital Travels Series

CAPITAL
BOOKS, INC.
Sterling, Virginia

Capital Books, Inc.
P.O. Box 605
Herndon, Virginia 20172-0605

ISBN 13: 978-1-933102-51-1

Library of Congress Cataloging-in-Publication Data

Stone, Suzanne, 1950-
Volunteering around the globe : life-changing travel adventures / Suzanne Stone.
p. cm. — (Capital travels series)
ISBN 978-1-933102-51-1 (alk. paper)
1. Travel. 2. Voluntarism. I. Title. II. Series.

G155.A1S6685 2008
361.3'7—dc22

2008002294

Printed in the United States of America on acid-free paper that meets the American National Standards Institute Z39-48 Standard.

First Edition

10 9 8 7 6 5 4 3 2 1

In honor of my parents,
Arthur and Ethel Stone,
who set the example,
and my children,
Adam Kramer and Miriam Kramer,
who are carrying it on.

Animal conservation.

CONTENTS

Section 3: Sources

PREFACE

I came home from my first "volunteer vacation" in 2005 energized and excited to tell people about the trip. Although it was my fourth trip to a country I thought I knew pretty well, especially since one trip was a year-long stay, I realized that I had gotten to know the country, its people, and culture more profoundly than during any other trip. I also realized that although I worked every day of the trip, I returned more rested and revitalized than from most of my previous vacations. I saw that I had been transformed and wanted others to know that they could have similar life-altering adventures.

I also realized that volunteer vacations, or "meaningful travel" as it is sometimes called, offers a new way to see the world. It is an alternative for people who have traveled extensively. When you volunteer in a country, you get to know it in a very different way. You return home with richer experiences and with greater insight into yourself.

On the other hand, I know people who have not traveled much, either because of the cost, or because they are bewildered by the enormity of planning a trip to a foreign country where people speak a different language and use different currency. I realized that volunteer vacations might be an answer for these people as well. Like tours, these vacations can be well planned and led by professionals who help navigate the new and strange sites. Yet, they can be much less expensive than tours or packaged holiday vacations.

I spoke with my publisher about writing a book about my volunteering experiences. She suggested including others' stories as well as my own, providing examples of the many ways people can volunteer around the globe. I looked into the topic of international volunteering and saw that the possibilities are almost inexhaustible. I also saw that, like me, you do not need any special education, background, or skills to volunteer anywhere in the world. You only need a desire to travel in a new way and an openness to the adventure.

THE TRANSFORMATIVE NATURE
OF VOLUNTEER VACATIONS

In the course of researching and writing this book, I interviewed twenty-three people and spoke with two of my friends, all of whom are enthusiastic about their experiences. Though each person or couple had a unique experience, I discovered many common points:

- Everyone found volunteering to be more meaningful than they thought it would be. The Petersons (whose stories are on pages 57, 99, 112, 115, and 133) say that their trips "have transformed our lives. We read a much broader range of books and are certainly more tolerant and appreciative of other cultures and what we can learn from them." A number of people spoke about learning of the power one person can have.
- Many people felt tested, and most discovered inner (and outer) strengths they did not know they possessed. Schuyler Richardson (whose stories are on pages 53 and 87) said one reason she took her trips was to go outside her comfort zone, to push herself, and not just physically. She says that she

was terrified during her Earthwatch adventure, but returned home "high for weeks" from learning what she was capable of.

▸ Most made lifelong friends. Janet McKelvey, who did disaster relief in Sri Lanka (page 83), talked about the wonderful friends she made, not only among the Sri Lankans, but also among her fellow volunteers, from both the United States and Great Britain. Gloria Gery, who has returned a number of times to volunteer in Romania (page 124), says she has made "lasting friendships with other volunteers, people I would never have met otherwise; people from all different lifestyles, careers and interests."

▸ Those who traveled with family members returned with stronger bonds and, as David Taylor and his son did, with greater appreciation for each other, a recognition of mutual support, and memories that will last their lifetimes (page 64).

▸ Many were moved by the conditions they saw and experienced in other countries, leading to a greater appreciation of their own lives, both for the ease and comfort that material goods provide, and also for the realization that such material goods are not always necessary for a happy and fulfilled life. The Hannas, who volunteered in Kenya (page 120), saw how grateful people with little are for just a bit more. They worked in an orphanage with children who lacked not only almost every object we take for granted, but also family members, yet were happy because they were better off now than they had been.

▸ We all discovered that people are just people, all over the world. Susan Colman, who taught law in Uganda (page 21), was struck repeatedly by how her students "were just like me. I was overwhelmed by the feeling that there were zero differences among us." As Bettie Peterson says, "Nothing has the impact of people interacting with people. We cannot go away unchanged. The ripple effect is hard to measure but I believe it is great."

As you can see, meaningful travel is transformative. Not only for the people whose lives you touch, but also for you.

Having realized this, I was not surprised when I read about one recent scientific experiment. Researchers at the National Institutes of Health examined the brains of people while they thought either about a scenario where they donated money to charity or about one where they kept the money for themselves. They found that when the people thought about giving the money away, a part of the brain was activated that usually is activated in response to food or sex, suggesting that there may be scientific evidence for the idea that doing good feels good. I do not think our altruistic feelings and generosity are solely a matter of brain chemistry, but it was interesting to see that modern science is confirming what many of us experienced. Giving has rewards for the giver as well as the recipient.

The rewards are so great that some people find this type of travel habit-forming; many of the volunteers I spoke with had gone on only one trip, but most of them were planning at least a second trip. I also spoke with people who have returned year after year to one place or who have taken as many as ten volunteer vacations, all to different locations and some with different organizations.

I met one woman whose "volunteer vacation" lasted one year and encompassed fourteen different experiences. Jane Stanfield had been planning on a fewer number, but when she was provided the means for a year off, she crafted her dream projects with seven organizations. She planned carefully, making sure she would be in each hemisphere and location for the best season and that she could travel relatively easily from one location to the next. Her year consisted of the following programs:

- Earthwatch—working on an archeological dig in Thailand, koala tracking in Australia, and exploring the lives of echidnas and goannas, also in Australia;
- Global Volunteers—working with orphans in Peru and Romania, teaching English in the Cook Islands;
- i-to-i Meaningful Travel—taking care of wallabies and tending eagles in Australia, and caring for lions in South Africa;
- Centre for Animal Rehabilitation and Education (CARE)—caring for baboons;
- Enkosini Wildlife Sanctuary—feeding and caring for penguins in South Africa;
- Pueblo Ingles—speaking conversational English in Spain;
- La Sabranenque—helping on historic reconstruction projects in France and Italy.

One of Jane's favorite sayings about travel is Hilaire Belloc's: "I have wandered all my life, and I have also traveled; the difference between the two being this, that we wander for distraction, but we travel for fulfillment."

WHO THIS BOOK IS FOR

This book is for anyone who is looking for a new way to travel:

- If you have traveled extensively and are looking for something different, this book is for you.
- If you have never traveled abroad yet want to, this book is for you.
- If you are looking for a less expensive way to travel, this book is for you.
- If you are looking for a way to experience another culture, this book is for you.
- If you are looking for a way to give something back, this book is for you.

This book can help you learn how to decide what trip to take, as well as provide information on practical matters for your travel. It contains stories of people just like you who have had the times of their lives volunteering around the globe.

Community development in Kenya.

HOW TO USE THIS BOOK

This book is designed to help you learn more about volunteer vacations, or meaningful travel as it is sometimes called.

The first section of the book provides:

▸ Guidelines about how to decide what trip to take
▸ Four stories of three atypical volunteer vacations
▸ Advice on practical travel-related matters and financing your trip.

This is followed by thirty-four more first-person stories about volunteer travel and vacations in the following activities:

▸ Business development
▸ Construction
▸ Cultural preservation
▸ Disaster relief
▸ Environmental work and conservation
▸ Healthcare
▸ Social services
▸ Teaching

My guess is you will be inspired to add meaningful travel to your life before you finish even half of the stories. But try to read them all, since they provide insight into the decision-making necessary for a successful trip. And as you read about others' adventures and the organizations that supported them, keep in mind the major decision-making questions:

- ▸ What do I want to do?
- ▸ Where do I want to go?
- ▸ Are there intriguing side trips I can take?
- ▸ How do I want to live during my program?
- ▸ What am I looking for from an organization?

The third section contains summaries of the ten organizations that sponsored the trips described in this book and two lists to help you navigate among these organizations. One list contains the countries that each of these organizations serves, and the other allows you to explore the opportunities each organization provides.

Remember: This book is by no means comprehensive. There are thousands of people experiencing this type of travel while you read this sentence and hundreds of organizations that sponsor such trips. The goal of this book is to show a variety of experiences, by type of activity, by country, and by type of individual. Another goal is to show that anyone can have a volunteer vacation. No special skills or talent are needed. Opportunities exist for people of any age, with any background. The only requirements are a desire to help and an openness to the adventure of self-transformation.

SECTION 1

Practical Advice

Ecology project.

CHAPTER 1

How to Decide What Trip to Take

In her book *Leap! What Will We Do with the Rest of Our Lives?*, Sara Davidson describes a volunteer vacation she took that did not work out very well. Her story shows how critical it is to match your personality, your strengths and weaknesses, and your desires with the right program, sponsored by the right organization.

The stories in this book are of people who made the right decision, matching their interests and needs with the right organization and adventure. Once you decide you want to take a volunteer vacation, there are a number of factors to consider:

▸ What you want to do and why
▸ What country or countries you want to visit
▸ The living situation you will be most comfortable in
▸ The length of the trip
▸ The cost
▸ The type of organization you want to go with
▸ Or even whether you want organizational support.

What You Want to Do

The types of activities open to volunteers are almost limitless. And for many, this is the starting point. Some people choose to do something they are familiar with—be it tending children, working in a kitchen, or painting homes.

Others jump at the opportunity to do something completely new—be it teaching English, building bridges, or caring for lion cubs. You can put professional experience to use in volunteering, or you can explore potential new careers. Consider also what your day as a volunteer will be like. Some projects require evening or nighttime work, while others are strictly nine to five. You may be working largely on your own or in a team.

This book contains stories of people who have volunteered in the most common types of projects:

> Business development—In many countries you can advise micro-businesses.

> Construction—Building in developing countries requires far more human labor than in the United States, and the demand is great for unskilled, as well as skilled, volunteers.

> Cultural preservation—Projects exist throughout the world, including in the United States, where you can help protect or restore languages, buildings, arts and crafts, or other aspects of cultural life.

> Disaster relief—Due to news stories of earthquakes, floods, tsunamis, and hurricanes, we all are unfortunately familiar with the type of work required to rebuild communities that have been ravaged by natural or man-made disaster. While immediate help is essential, in many cases, disaster relief work continues for years.

> Environmental work and conservation—A growing number of organizations offer opportunities to maintain parks and other public spaces, restore habitats, assist in scientific research, or help in distinct conservation efforts, such as protecting sea turtle populations, as Stephanie Kwong did (page 90); tracking spiny anteaters, as Muriel Horacek

did (page 85); or helping plant trees in Nepal, as Adam Forbes did (page 101).

‣ Healthcare and social services—Impoverished countries have a tremendous need for healthcare and other social services, which can be delivered to children, the elderly, or people of all ages with disabilities.

‣ Teaching —One of the most common volunteer projects is helping teach English, as Liz O'Callahan did in Thailand (page 24). However, many other subjects can be taught, as Kelly Ferguson learned in her experience in Kenya (page 130).

You also need to examine why you want to volunteer. The people who return with the greatest satisfaction were motivated not merely to accomplish some good in the world, but also to learn about the world and about themselves. Even if you choose an activity similar to your

i-to-i Meaningful Travel

Volunteer teaching.

current field and travel with friends or relatives, you need to be prepared for moving outside your comfort zone. Your trip will demand that you stretch and in doing so, grow. You will be challenged. And while people will appreciate what you have done, you need to know that the true satisfaction will come from your own sense of accomplishment, not from anyone else's gratitude.

What Country or Countries You Want to Visit

The choice of locations—both countries and settings—can be daunting and plays a very big part in what type of experience you will have. You can go almost anywhere in the world. For some people, the starting point for meaningful travel is choosing a part of the world they want to travel to. This may be down the street, as it is for Christa Lyons (page 26), within the U.S., or halfway around the world.

You may want to be situated in a city, small town, rural area, or the great outdoors. Some people, like Laura Silver (page 49), appreciate the opportunity to live in a completely different setting; she traveled from midtown Manhattan to a small town in Senegal. Others want something more familiar, even if that means only traveling from a city to a city. Keep in mind that the cities you are likely to travel to are probably quite different from the city you live in, so it won't be exactly like home.

Projects in cities and those in rural areas tend to be quite different. Most conservation projects, for example, are located outside of large cities. Many social service projects, on the other hand, are in cities or small towns. In addition, your ability to immerse yourself in another culture may depend on the location. There are no hard and fast rules on this, however. It is largely dependent as well on the type of work you will do and your living arrangements. For example, while conservation efforts in the great outdoors will probably expose you to the fewest number of people, you may still become very familiar with the country and its culture through your project and through the scientists you work with or the family you stay with.

Finally, be sure to consider the weather as well as the country's culture and language in making your choice. Be honest about whether you prefer hot or cold, rainy or sunny, mountains or valleys, or something in between.

You might want to pick a place you have always dreamed of visiting. Many volunteers tie in a side trip during the weekends or on their way home. Lots of people who travel to Africa include a safari on their trip. The Petersons visited New Zealand after volunteering in the Cook Islands, and the Galapagos after a volunteer stint in Ecuador. They have chosen a different location for each of their many volunteer trips.

For a first trip, if you are feeling a bit timid, pick something close to home. My friends Alan and Helene Kahan (page 82) chose a short trip to New Orleans, where their children were working with AmeriCorps. Barb Everhart (pages 70 and 78) and Schuyler Richardson (pages 53 and 87) both chose travel in the United States before they ventured to foreign lands. That's what Jane Stanfield—the person who carved out a year-long adventure—suggests: "To find out if a volunteer vacation is right for you, take a short trip preferably in the United States, so you can get a taste of the experience."

If you want to leave the United States but would rather start your adventure in an English-speaking country, there are many to choose from.

You might pick a place that you think you can't afford. As discussed on pages 11-13, volunteering may offer a less expensive way to travel.

Living Situation

Living situations vary widely and can be a critical factor in your decision making. Many programs include home stays, which can be an extension of the cultural immersion experience. Some people don't appreciate home stays, feeling a loss of privacy and freedom that is even more important in unfamiliar settings. Others love it. John Donegan, who taught in Ghana (page 104), valued his home stay with a family, describing the opportunity to become part of a local family as a "privilege." Sara Spike also valued her opportunity to live with a family in Tanzania (page 109). She not only appreciated the opportunity it provided her to learn but also to extend her contributions: she helped teach the family English during her five-week stay, and she learned that the fees paid to the family provided them with the means to acquire running water. It's important that you try to imagine whether you would be comfortable with a home stay.

Other programs provide private accommodations, and these can range from the primitive to fairly comfortable housing of three- or four-star hotel quality. Gloria Gery chose her project in part because it included private accommodations at a local hotel (page 124). She believed that after spending a full day tending to children, interacting with the clinic's staff, and getting to know other volunteers, she would need some quiet "alone time." This was obviously part of the right decision for her, because she has returned many times to the clinic. Muriel Horacek, on the other hand, says accommodations are not important to her. During her thirty-five Earthwatch trips (page 85), she has "stayed in just about every type of accommodation, from a private room in a nice hotel in the Czech Republic to a cave in China."

Perhaps most common is group housing. Just like private accommodations, these can range from fairly primitive to fairly comfortable. Stephanie Kwong, who went on a project to help save turtles in Costa Rica (page 90), loved the camp-like nature of her accommodations: a two-story hut without running water. Although surprised by the roughness, she was also delighted. But not everyone would be. So, if you have any qualms about the living conditions of any project, check them out thoroughly with the sponsoring organization. Many volunteers appreciate the ability to make closer friends with the others on their trip while living in group housing. Sarah Forman, who traveled to Russia (page 119), found staying together in one hotel provided more opportunities to make friends with her fellow volunteers. Others may find that this type of living condition interferes with opportunities to meet the local people, learn the local language, or further immerse yourself in the local culture.

Finally, consider who else may be living or working with you. Family members often, but not always, take these trips together. None of the organizations profiled in this book have an upper age limit, and many allow children when accompanied by adult family members. David Taylor went to Tanzania with his thirteen-year-old son and is now considering additional trips with his younger children as each nears adolescence. Many of the programs I write about are based in the United States, and it appears that the typical group consists mostly of North Americans. However, organizations based in other countries will provide a different mix of nationalities.

As discussed above, your work environment will depend in large part on what activity you will do. You could find yourself in an office setting or a school or outdoors. You need to consider the off-hours as well. If the project requires work only in the daytime or for five days in the week, check out what opportunities there are for evening and weekend activities. Will you be spending the evenings with your fellow volunteers, getting to know your host family, or choosing your own activity—whether it's exploring your new city or resting quietly? What places will you be near for weekend trips, and does your organization help arrange travel?

Do not forget to consider food. In some projects, the volunteers and local staff buy and cook their meals. In others, the host family or hotel provides the meals. No matter who prepares them, the meals will be largely of local cuisine.

Length of the Trip

Most programs offer trips of two to four weeks in length, but you can volunteer for shorter or longer periods of time. In some projects, volunteers can sign up for months. Jane Stanfield designed an entire year of volunteering in different countries. She wanted to get hands-on experience, especially with animals, so she joined projects in South America, Australia, and South Africa that fulfilled that desire. She also traveled to Europe and the South Pacific, doing activities as varied as teaching English and working on an archeological dig.

Most short-term projects are part of larger efforts, so if completion of a project is critical to you, be sure to

Global Volunteers

A volunteer construction project in Costa Rica.

find out what you and your team will accomplish in your few weeks. You may be satisfied knowing that you helped build a road that others will finish or that you and your new friends completed the rehabbing of one new home for a family.

Cost

Most organizations charge a fee, which includes lodging, meals, and in-country travel. These fees often include orientation, language training, and other educational programs and help cover the costs of salaries for host country staff and the organization's operating expenses. Make sure you know what's included in terms of language instruction, pre-departure information and support, and in-country orientation and support; if these are important to you, they could well be worth the necessary fees.

The fees also may include health insurance, emergency medical and evacuation insurance, and international phone service. If not, it is strongly recommended that you provide these for yourself. In addition, you will be responsible for air travel and, if not covered by the fees, passport and visa fees, and nonwork travel and tours.

Be sure to calculate the total cost of the projects you are considering. Lower fees do not necessarily always mean that the project will be the least expensive one. If you need to pay for health insurance and an international telephone, those costs plus the fees may end up being more than the fees for a program that include insurance and telephones.

At first glance, many people ask why a fee is involved. As explained above, these fees cover not only your local expenses while on a project but also help fund the organization. The majority of groups sponsoring this type of vacation are not-for-profit organizations, whose chief sources of funding are donations by individuals. Even with the fee factored in, the total cost of a volunteer vacation can be less than paying individual rates for hotels and dining.

Lowering the Cost

You may be able to raise the funds that will cover your program fee. This can be as simple as asking your friends and relatives to make a contribution to the organization. Global Citizens Network (GCN), for instance, describes how some of its volunteers have raised funds successfully. One, who went to Kenya, sent a letter to family, friends, and "just about every person or acquaintance" she could think of. In the letter, she explained GCN's mission, the project, and her intentions. A few months later she sent out postcards to remind people of the deadline. She found that many people enjoyed living vicariously through her endeavors. Her donors responded to her inspiring quotation by Gandhi: "Be the change you want to see in the world." She explained, "If I don't care enough to change the things that are important, how can I possibly expect anyone else to?"

Fundraising can involve more elaborate efforts. Some people write letters to companies and foundations, outlining both their project and the overall work of the organization. The request for funding should describe how the donation will make an impact on the community or program where you will be volunteering. Requests to civic and religious organizations can include the offer to make a presentation about your trip to the organization's members. It's a good idea, whether you make such a presentation or not, to both thank your funders and stay in touch with them with progress reports during and after your trip.

If you're interested in raising funds for your travel, be sure to check with the organizations you're exploring to see if they allow it and whether they provide any guidance.

In addition, your supporters' donations and a portion of your costs might be tax-deductible, which further lowers the total cost. The Internal Revenue Service allows you to deduct donations to U.S. nonprofit organizations. These donations may include some of the program fees as well as at least a portion of the travel costs. Two key factors must be considered in determining whether travel expenses to and from a long-distance volunteer location are deductible. One is the amount of time that is spent volunteering. Another is how direct your travel is to and from the location of your volunteer project. A 1986 Tax Act does not allow deduction for travel expenses if you spend a significant amount of personal pleasure or recreation time before, during, or after your volunteer activities. You will need to discuss the possibility of these deductions with your tax advisor.

The Type of Organization

One final consideration is the sponsoring organization. Most of the ones that support meaningful travel are nonprofit organizations, also known as not-for-profit organizations, or—primarily outside the United States—as non-governmental organizations (NGO). Nonprofit organizations exist to benefit a local community or the nation. Their activities generally are charitable or educational in nature. These organizations are not owned nor do they operate to provide financial gain to owners or anyone else. They can have large operating budgets, as does the International Red Cross, or operate on much leaner funding. Many of the smaller nonprofits use volunteers as well as paid staff. For these reasons, the United States Internal Revenue Service grants them status as exempt from income taxes. Some for-profit business and corporations also sponsor meaningful travel.

Most likely, factors other than the tax status of an organization will be more important in determining whether you select an organization, such as:

▸ The type of projects the organization sponsors. Most organizations conduct service or self-help programs.

▸ The organization's history. You may want to know how long the organization has been in business, whether it's growing, and at what rate, and how it may have changed focus over time.

▸ Whether projects are cosponsored with local partners. Some organizations have a strong philosophy of allowing local organizations to take the lead in determining country needs and projects. In some cases, this can contribute to the need for flexibility once on site.

▸ How much "free time" is provided and whether educational programs or local travel are included. Some organizations offer more learning opportunities than others.

▸ What type and how much support are provided, both before and during the projects. Check out whether the organization helps choose the most suitable trip for you; provides pre-departure advice about international travel and about your destination and work project, including in-country education or assistance; and offers help in emergencies.

As you consider a volunteer vacation, it may be helpful to make a list of questions. I suggest you start with the following:

1. What type of work do I want to do?
2. What part of the world or what country do I want to go to?
3. Is the climate or topography critical to me?
4. Do I care if I live in a city, small town, or rural area?

5. What living arrangements do I want? And how important are they to me?
6. What can I afford? Am I willing to raise funds for part of the fees?
7. How much support do I need, before I go and while I am away?
8. Why do I want to do this? Be honest about your goals and motives.

Now, read through the stories in this book and study the organizations' profiles. Go online to search out more about these organizations and others. Be sure to check out schedules for the programs that interest you to see if they match your availability.

Choose two to four projects and/or organizations. Next, make a list of questions for the staff and past volunteers. Include some of the questions in Chapter Three, "Practical Matters."

Contact the organizations and ask your questions. Find out if you can speak with past volunteers to question them directly about the projects that interest you.

Choose a program and begin the application. Next thing you know, you will be on a fabulous, life-altering adventure!

Tanzanian children.

CHAPTER 2

Atypical Trips

Most of the stories in this book feature people who chose to volunteer through an organization and who selected projects that did not draw on their professional skills. But there are other routes to meaningful travel. You can go without organizational support. And you can apply your professional background to the experience. Finally, you do not need to travel far away for the transformative trip of your life.

Without Organizational Support

It may be, as Sara Davidson concluded about herself in her book *Leap! What Will We Do with the Rest of Our Lives?*, that you will not want to volunteer with any organization but want to perform, as she calls it, "wing-it-yourself style of service." And I understand that well; that's what I have done. I knew I wanted to give back to a country that is personally meaningful, Israel. So I did an Internet search, using "volunteer" and "Israel" as my search terms. I learned about *Livnot U'Lehibanot* (www.livnot.org.il), a program designed for people like me who have a desire to help in Israel, but don't know where to start. I arranged my own housing by renting an apartment in Jerusalem.

One of this organization's main activities is conducting tours for groups, usually of people under age thirty. These tours always include a few days of volunteering. The permanent staff also works on a variety of projects to alleviate poverty in Israel, and volunteers like myself are welcome to join in. The organization's name means "to build and to be built," which describes its philosophy that through helping build a community, the volunteer is built as well. St. Francis of Assisi also said it, "In giving, we receive."

Through the Livnot staff, I was sent to a soup kitchen, where I spent my mornings peeling and chopping vegetables, and helping cook chicken, soup, and potatoes. Early afternoons, I set tables, served lunches, and helped clean.

The soup kitchen where I worked was part of Hazon Yeshaya or Isaiah's Vision (www.hazonyeshaya.org), a network of kitchens founded by a businessman kept alive as a child by soup kitchens in Paris, when he and his family were refugees from Egypt. People of all nationalities, backgrounds, races and religions are fed by *Hazon Yeshaya*, which distributes meals to over 7,000 people daily from more than thirty-eight locations. In the kitchen where I volunteered, 2,400 nutritious lunches a day were sent to schools and daycare centers, about 200 people were served at the center, and another 500 meals were delivered to people's homes.

Suzanne Stone working in soup kitchen.

During my stay, I also visited victims of terror, co-ordinated by One Family Fund (www.onefamilyfund.org). I met children whose fathers and siblings had been killed, a mother whose son was killed in a café bombing, a young wife and mother of seven whose husband had a break-down and abandoned his family, and a young Christian woman from the Ukraine who was injured in a bomb blast on a bus when she was ten weeks pregnant (during that visit, I played with the daughter who had been in her womb during the blast and was miraculously uninjured).

Describing my volunteer activities is less than half the story. As the Livnot agency knows only too well, these acts were not totally unselfish; I received far more than I gave on this trip.

At the soup kitchen, I met many wonderful people—other volunteers, staff, and "the regulars." At first, I was reluctant to serve meals because I wanted my actions to be anonymous. Over time, I grew to enjoy serving because I got to know many of the regulars and realized that the kitchen provides them with more than food. It's a place to socialize with friends, and I became a new friend to chat with and eventually—as my Hebrew improved—even to tease and joke with.

Visiting families affected by terror was awe-inspiring. It is impossible to appreciate these survivors' strengths without firsthand witness. Learning about the work con-ducted by foundations and agencies in Israel also was hum-bling. Most people don't realize the country's high poverty rate or fully comprehend the impact of years of terrorist attacks.

Thus, my first "volunteer vacation," in late 2005, changed me in many ways. This book—my first—is one of those transformations. Most of the other changes are a bit more profound. I began to understand what is necessary for personal growth and for true fulfillment. Breaking out of your routine can be both a real vacation and also an

Suzanne Stone

Volunteers and paid staff at Hazon Yeshaya.

exercise in confidence building. Focusing on other people is a great start toward self-fulfillment. Realizing that the smallest of positive actions has consequences for others and for yourself can provide a renewed purpose to one's life. And I finally profoundly understood that what some see as charity and therefore define as altruistic or unselfish is simply what we are meant to do to help repair the world. I am grateful to all the people who allowed me to perform this obligation.

Professional Volunteering

While a key message of this book is that anyone can volunteer and no special skills are needed, sometimes people find it most fulfilling to offer "professional volunteering," using their training and skills to help others. As I worked on this book, I realized that one of my friends fit this category. Here is her story.

Susan Colman

In the spring of 2003, a dear friend approached me for what turned out to be the trip that changed my life. This man, who is an attorney and the husband of a retired federal judge, is also on the board of directors of the International Senior Lawyers Project (ISLP). He e-mailed me two questions: "Do you know much about e-commerce?" and "Would you like to go to Uganda?" My response was "I'm packed; when do you want me to go?"

The ISLP worked at that time with the International Law Institute (ILI) in Kampala, Uganda, to develop some courses that would be taught by lawyers from the United States. Three lawyers from the Washington, D.C., area comprised the first groups of teachers. One left in August 2003 and one in September; they taught courses on corporate governance and antitrust law. I went in October and taught a five-day course on legal aspects of e-commerce. It took me five months to prepare for the project, during which time I developed a 600-650 page compendium of laws, articles, and other materials for the class.

Eight students—all lawyers except for one contract specialist—attended the course. I chose to run the class very informally. We put our desks into a circle. Also I can be very funny. I told the class at the beginning that I was an intellectual with a great sense of humor, and that we'd be laughing all week. Later, ILI staff members told me that whenever they walked outside my classroom that week, they heard laughter. I taught for five or six hours each day. With lunch and two delightful Ugandan tea breaks, I worked an eight-hour day. But my day—and the fun—didn't stop there. After class, the students and I would stay and talk . . . and laugh some more.

Students came from Zambia and Tanzania, as well as Uganda and Kenya. They had very different backgrounds and different tribal origins and spoke at least two different languages as well as English. As a linguaphile, I really took advantage of this opportunity to learn about all these various languages. I learned that many people in Africa speak at least three languages: their tribal language, their national language, and the language of the country that had once colonized their land.

I found it very moving that as we talked among ourselves, whatever preconceptions we might have had about one another were just blown away. I was different from any American they had met or heard about or had preconceptions of. And they were just like me. I was overwhelmed by the feeling that there were zero differences among us. I experienced many magical moments where I would think, "This is what the world should be like." This is not to say that we agreed about everything. For example, in one of our class discussions about the employer's legal

International Law Institute staff

Susan Colman (front center) with her class and ILI staff in the courtyard at the Institute.

right to review employees' e-mails, one student was very outraged and argued strongly with me and other class members. Later, however, we were able to laugh about our different attitudes. In a way, we were like a family; certainly family members do not always agree with one another. In fact, everyone treated me like I was a long-lost family member and treated me with almost instant friendship and warmth.

What affected me the most on this trip is that even though I felt somewhat conspicuous, I was embraced as if I were one of them. The people were so friendly, so open, and so welcoming. I have been told that, like everywhere else, there are plenty of selfish and mean people in African countries, but I never saw or met any. And to some extent, I have been "Africanized." One of the two students with whom I stay in touch says he cannot tell me apart from his sisters even though I am old enough to be his mother. I am an adopted member of his family and am getting a name in Kunda (his family's tribal language). That really enhances my feeling that we are all one world, that all people are really part of one big tribe.

I am usually never at a loss for words, but often discover when I try to describe Africa that I can't find the words. Even remembering my experience just takes my breath away. I have been both overwhelmed and transformed by my experience. When I got on the airplane to leave, I just cried. And the only thing that keeps that sadness at bay is knowing that I'm going back.

Another lawyer who volunteered with ISLP, Jim Dube, states, "On a personal note, my volunteer experience working with Liberia 's Ministry of Justice was both an awakening and a wake-up call. There are many lawyers throughout North America who are either nearing retirement or retired, but who still have much to contribute. The need for legal skills is so great in nations like Liberia. Yet, I believe that many of us hesitate to volunteer because we create self-imposed limits on what we think we can accomplish—limits driven by our experience in practicing law. Certainly in my case, I wondered how an Ontario litigator with a background in financial institutions and insolvency restructuring work could provide useful help to the challenges being faced by Liberia 's Ministry of Justice. The truth is that, with reasonably good minds and a preparedness to venture beyond our comfort boundaries, our generation of lawyers has an enormous capacity to make a difference. And, it is organizations like International Senior Lawyers Project that enable us to do so."

Liz O'Callahan

As I worked on this book, I met Liz O'Callahan, who has returned to volunteer in a country where she studied. Here is her story.

Two years ago, I did a study abroad program in Northeast Thailand that brought me into the lives and homes of people in the region. It was based in Khon Kaen, a regional capital. I always knew I wanted to come back to visit the people here, but never thought I would be returning to do any kind of work. However, when the Educational Network for Grassroots and Global Exchange (ENGAGE)—a network of alumni from the study abroad program in which I participated—sent an e-mail over its listserve about the opportunity to teach in Khon Kaen, I decided to apply for the program. I felt the best way to give back to the community I had studied with would be to take a job working with the local people, helping to build something with them. In this case, it is a way of looking at education and a system for making it work better.

I am now working with a program called the Khon Kaen Education Initiative (KKEI), run by an organization called Thai Seeka. It is currently in its first stage; I am one of the first seven people to come and work with English teachers in Khon Kaen. Right now, a lot is trial and error.

As a part of the initial group of participants, part of my job is to help build a sustainable structure under which we can all operate.

KKEI is trying to build a structure under which local municipal teachers can benefit from the knowledge of native English speakers. This means that I, along with six other volunteer teachers, am working on improving the English language abilities of Thai English teachers and increasing their confidence in that ability.

I work in a classroom four days a week to help teach or observe teaching, taking notes on what aspects need improvement (pronunciation, grammar, kids not comprehending the lessons, etc.). I also spend significant time scripting lesson plans that teachers can use to prepare something specific without relying on translation. The idea is that students expecting a Thai translation will never learn to listen to the English. I spend a good deal of time in meetings as well and meet with other participants, both the international teachers and the whole KKEI team (Thai and international teachers) weekly. We discuss how the teaching process is progressing, logistics that should be addressed, the best way to promote the program, etc.

I am currently living with two of the other international participants in a house that the Thai teachers found for us. I receive a monthly housing stipend that, under this set-up, pays for housing and utilities. The stipend/salary I receive as a volunteer (actually, that title might change very soon to "employee" for visa reasons), will cover all of my needs in Thailand and my roundtrip airfare from the U.S., as well as provide a little money for travel within the country.

It's very different being here as a volunteer as opposed to a tourist. First, almost no one comes to Khon Kaen for tourism; it's simply not a Thai tourist site. There are no beaches, no hill tribes, and very few elephants. I also am much more connected to daily life than a tourist would be. All the people I know here are teachers or work in education in some way. It's also different from my study abroad experience because I'm not going out to experience the rural culture. The people I interact with are city dwellers, not villagers, and primarily middle class, not poor.

I expected a lot of what I am experiencing; I knew it was a new program that can be unpredictable. I knew it would be a process where I would be working from a bottom-up rather than top-down perspective. Originally, I didn't know what it was going to mean to be a teacher. I thought I would be doing more direct teaching of students and might have my own classes. Instead, I work primarily with teachers and assist them in their classrooms to varying degrees, depending upon the teacher I work with.

Yet there are some unexpected aspects to my experience: I did not anticipate the problems that come from working under a government system with people who have worked primarily in the private sector. Very few people know how to deal with the Thai government system. I also did not expect a military coup to occur while I was here, or the changes in visa regulations (especially for teachers) that would come when a man, teaching in Thai schools, claimed to be JonBenet Ramsey's killer.

Close to Home

You may not want to travel far to volunteer. Fortunately, there are transformative ways to volunteer at home, some of them even offer "virtual" ways to see the world. Consider the story of one retiree in Northern Virginia:

Christa Lyons

September 11th, 2001, changed the course of my life and that of many immigrants. I had just retired from thirty years in the federal government and was looking forward to volunteering with the Humane Society of the United States or World Wildlife. I love animals. But, like so many others, after 9/11, I found myself drawn to the Red Cross. "I just have to do something to help" was my dominant thought.

While at the local Red Cross chapter, only one block from my home, the trajectory of my plans swerved in an unforeseen direction; I wound up helping in ways far removed from the 9/11 disaster. I read about the Red Cross's International Services. I think everyone knows that the Red Cross helps people whenever and wherever natural or man-made disaster strikes. But in addition to helping in the immediate aftermath of an earthquake, tsunami, or terrorist attack, the Red Cross offers longer-range services. One of these is the Holocaust and War Victims Tracing Center.

Since 1945, the Red Cross and affiliated societies around the world have been tracing people separated from family members during war or civil unrest. This program, which has become so much of my life now, has three goals: to locate missing loved ones, exchange messages among these people, and make disaster relief inquiries.

Perhaps I was attracted to this program because I was born in an internment camp (my parents were German nationals running a leper colony in Nigeria during World War II and were interned by the British in 1940. My parents had left Germany in 1938 for their work in Nigeria). My father's grandfather was born Jewish and as a result, my father's father was put to death in Auschwitz. But for whatever reason, in the past six years, I have worked thirty to forty hours each week helping to reunite families from various war-torn countries in Africa. Without going geographically very far from my home, I have metaphorically traveled many times to Sierra Leone, Somalia, Ethiopia, Eritrea, and many other countries.

How it works is that someone comes to the Red Cross to request that we search for his or her family member back home in Africa. I interview the person three or four times, seeking to help the individual remember as many details as he or she can about life back home. The smallest clues can be the tipping point. For example, one memorable case I worked on is that of Katie, who as a young girl in Sierra Leone watched her mother board the local bus on a buying trip for her fruit and vegetable stand, normally a routine trip but this time one from which she never returned. Later Katie saw on television that the bus had been attacked by rebels. She did not know what happened to her mother.

A few years later the rebel forces broke into Katie's home. She and her brother were forced to watch and even applaud as the insurgents burned their home and killed their father, who was trapped inside. After several months with the rebels, Katie and her brother became refugees, first in Guinea and then in Ghana. They eventually made their way to the United States. Katie sought our services, and from one tiny fact that she eventually remembered—the name of one shopkeeper her mother had been friends with—we were able to discover that Katie's mother is alive and well. One of my most satisfying days was the one when we put mother and daughter in touch with each other.

We take clues like this and every piece of data we can compile and fill out the "tracing inquiry forms." We then send the information to the National Headquarters of the American Red Cross where staff transmit them to the International Committee of the Red Cross, in Geneva, and from there to as many of the 180 Red Cross and Red Crescent societies and the Magen David Adom in Israel as necessary to begin the search. Information then starts to flow back and forth on this route for as long as it takes to close a case, hopefully with the discovery of a loved one still alive. This usually takes one to four years. We provide updates to the inquirer every six months or so.

The vast majority of our cases work in reverse. That is, we receive the tracing inquiry forms that have originated in a foreign country by someone who believes that his or her relatives might be in the United States. Our first step in these cases is to set up a case file with a road map of priority checklist activities to undertake. I am pleased that this checklist, which my chapter developed five years ago, is displayed by the American Red Cross on their website as a "best practice." This guides us in our search through the immigrant communities in Northern Virginia.

We use public records in our search. Everyone knows that the Internet contains a wealth of data. I am so happy when we can use this to help reunite loved ones. Names—especially last names—are one of our biggest clues. We will search telephone listings and other published records and then try to speak with everyone with the same last name, just to see if there is any connection. One of my most successful types of searches is visiting apartment managers. My colleagues and I always go armed with lots of Red Cross literature so we can educate the manager about our purpose. Invariably, as soon as he or she knows we can be trusted, the manager helps out. They sometimes tell us if the people we are seeking still live there, and other times they serve as a go-between. Every little step helps. Our most valued resources include local community leaders serving the various immigrant communities. So many immigrants do not trust any agency; their past experiences have taught them to be as wary of nongovernmental organizations as they are of governmental ones. However, they do trust leaders of their local immigrant community, and as soon as these community leaders learn to trust us, doors magically open.

Our successes mean so much to me. One of the most exciting cases also was one of the fastest; it took only six months to discover that a young immigrant's father, who had been deported from Ethiopia as a result of the conflict between Ethiopia and Eritrea, was alive and well back home in Ethiopia. In another case, we helped a native from

Sierra Leone, who had not seen her brother for twenty years, locate him here in Virginia.

It's hard to imagine what my life would be like if I had not taken that fateful trip to the local Red Cross six years ago. I shudder to think that some of the families I have helped reunite might not have found one another because the Red Cross was lacking in volunteers. More importantly, I cannot envisage how much poorer my life would be without this new sense of purpose and the many new friends I have made among staff, other volunteers, community members, and the immigrants.

CHAPTER 3

Practical Matters Before You Go

by Pamela Jones

You have made the decision to take a volunteer vacation. Now what do you have to do before you leave? The answer is a lot of things. First, learn as much as you can about your destination. Then, you need to make your travel plans. You also have to consider what will be available at your destination and what you need to take with you. The better prepared you are before you leave, the better off you will be.

If you're volunteering in the U.S., your preparations will be relatively simple. But if your destination is international, you have much to do.

Either way, the organization you're traveling with should provide orientation materials. The information here will both supplement that and provide a framework for asking more questions of the organization.

Where Are You Going?

Before setting out on your adventure, learn as much as possible about the country where you will be volunteering. Your first source of information will be the agency for which you will be volunteering. Find out as much as possible about the area. Becoming familiar with your destination will help maximize your experience and add to your enjoyment. It also helps pave the way to relationships with local residents.

HISTORY, CULTURE, AND CUSTOMS

Wherever you're traveling, start with the bigger picture and learn the country's history. Learning about the past will give you the background to start understanding a country's laws, customs, culture, and people. This information can be culled from any number of sources: your local public library, the Internet, and bookstores.

You'll find reference books and travel guides at your local library and bookstores, as well as at online bookstores. An online search of your destination country will lead you to government tourism sites, travel guides, and websites set up by individuals who have traveled there themselves. News articles and local newspapers are also available on the Internet. In addition, most travel guides now have websites.

The U.S. State Department offers "Background Notes" on every country with which the U.S. maintains diplomatic relations. These contain facts about each country's people, history, government, political conditions, economy, and foreign relations. These can be accessed by going to www.state.gov and clicking on "Countries" and then "Background Notes."

CURRENT SITUATION

Even more important than the history of your destination country is the current political, economic, and cultural climate. Has there been a recent change in government or are elections pending? Is unemployment at a high or low? What, if any, national or religious holidays might occur during your stay?

The organization sponsoring your trip should provide basic information, but a variety of sources can offer more. Check for articles in newspapers, both U.S. and international (i.e., the *New York Times*, *London Times,* and the *Financial Times*) and news magazines (i.e., *Time, Newsweek,* and the *Economist*). BBC World Service offers radio coverage of international events and is available over some public radio stations in the U.S. and on the BBC website (www.bbc.co.uk/radio/). A quick search of the Internet can also provide helpful information.

Via its Consular Information Service, the U.S. State Department has three components that provide information about travel to specific countries—Consular Information Sheets, Travel Warnings, and Public Announcements.

▸ Consular Information Sheets are available on more than 200 countries and have details on entry requirements, crime and security conditions, areas of instability, road safety, etc.

▸ Travel Warnings are issued when the State Department deems the situation in a country to be dangerous to U.S. citizens (e.g., civil unrest or terrorist activities); travel warnings often recommend that travel be cancelled or postponed. Such warnings can also be issued for countries with which the U.S. has no diplomatic relations, making it difficult for the U.S. government to assist citizens who encounter problems there.

▸ Public Announcements contain information about terrorist threats and short-term or transnational conditions that could affect U.S. travelers. These are all updated frequently and can be accessed at: www.travel.state.gov.

The State Department recommends that all U.S. citizens traveling abroad register with the State Department. This free service enables the State Department to contact a traveler regarding anything from a family emergency to a crisis in your destination country. You can register online at: https://travelregistration.state.gov

People who have visited the area recently are probably the best sources for information on your destination country. Try to talk with people who have volunteered recently with the program you are interested in or at least who have traveled to the same country. Ask them about their experiences.

THINGS TO REMEMBER

When visiting another country, you are subject to its laws. Become familiar with them and with the culture. Cultural influences, such as religious beliefs or politics, influence the legal system. Things that are perfectly acceptable in one country are illegal in others. For example, a number of years ago, an American friend visiting Greece was arrested for having a patch depicting the U.S. flag on her jeans. Recently, news stories have illustrated other examples where behavior that is acceptable in the U.S. has resulted in arrests and even punishments and deportations.

Some people forget to consider the dietary norms in the country they will visit. This is especially important if you have any food allergies. If you are allergic to shellfish or peanuts, for example, and are visiting a country where either of these are a major dietary staple, you should plan accordingly.

Money

Fees for almost all sponsored volunteer vacations include basic living expenses. But you will want to have money for sightseeing and any emergencies that might arise. How much should you take and in what form? You will have to decide how much "mad money" to allocate for your own side trips and shopping.

Should you take U.S. dollars or traveler's checks, or convert cash before you leave? While traveler's checks are usually considered safer than cash, they are not accepted universally. The organization should have this information, or you can check with your destination country's U.S. embassy or consulate. If you opt for traveler's checks, remember to write down the serial numbers and store them separately from the checks so you can have them replaced if they're lost or stolen. It is a good idea to leave a copy of the serial numbers with a friend or relative in the U.S., as well, so you have access to the numbers in case of an emergency.

Generally, it is wisest to have a relatively small amount of money, enough to get you through the first day or so, in local currency either when you arrive at your destination or soon thereafter. This will give you an opportunity to check fees from several sources to maximize the rest of your exchange. If you have not converted that amount before you leave, you can do so on arrival at a money exchange bureau in the airport. In most countries, money exchange bureaus offer rates that are competitive with or better than banks and are much quicker. Unless it is an emergency, do not exchange cash at a hotel; fees there are almost always the highest.

To determine the current exchange rate before you go, check with your bank or credit union or go online. A number of Internet sites provide currency exchange information: e.g., www.gocurrency.com, http://www.oanda.com

ATM machines now are available in most countries and offer the most convenience. However, bank exchange fees tend to be quite high—5 to 10 percent—so you may want to use this option sparingly.

Keeping cash, traveler's checks, and other documents safe when traveling is a major concern. The simplest and most conventional method is a "cash belt." This is a wallet with a strap that wraps around your waist that you wear underneath your clothing while traveling. Once you arrive at your destination, if you're staying at a hotel, it most likely will offer secure storage for your money and documentation at no charge.

You should seriously consider leaving any valuables such as jewelry or electronics at home.

Language

What language is spoken in your destination country? Although your volunteer organization probably will have English-speaking staff to work with you, find out whether you will you be able to communicate effectively with local residents in English.

Even if it isn't necessary, you may want to learn at least the basics of the local language to maximize your experience. Many options are available for learning another language, from evening programs at local community colleges or universities to audio courses that can be purchased online or in bookstores.

How Do You Get There?

What is the best way to reach your destination? Some volunteer organizations help with travel planning, but most leave it up to you.

Global Volunteers

Volunteer project in Tanzania.

You can work with a travel agent or utilize any of the many online travel sites. Among the most popular Internet sites for booking travel are:

▸ www.travelocity.com
▸ www.cheaptickets.com
▸ www.expedia.com
▸ www.travelzoo.com

Another option is to visit specific airline websites. If your destination country is not a developed country, this may be your best choice.

Be advised, when booking international travel, it often is necessary to provide your passport number (and, depending upon your destination country, visa number) to secure your reservation.

Passports and Visas

Depending upon your destination country, you will need a passport and possibly a visa. Passports are internationally recognized documents that establish the bearer's identity and nationality and are required for travel to most countries outside the U.S. There are more than 9,000 passport application acceptance centers; these include post offices and many federal, state, and probate courts; some pubic libraries; and a number of county and municipal offices. There are also thirteen regional passport agencies and a special "Gateway City Agency" that can assist those who are traveling within two weeks. These agencies require appointments; locations and hours can be found at http://travel.state.gov/passport/about/agencies/agencies_913.html.

Passport applications must include two photos, a birth certificate or other proof of U.S. citizenship, and a valid photo ID. You can generally apply for a new passport by mail if your most recent passport is undamaged and can be submitted with your application.

You must apply for a passport in person if:

▸ you are applying for a passport for the first time
▸ your expired passport is not in your possession
▸ your previous passport has expired and was is-sued more than fifteen years ago
▸ your previous passport was issued when you were fifteen or younger, or
▸ your currently valid U.S. passport has been lost or stolen.

At the time of publication of this book, the passport application fee, if you are sixteen or older, is $67 plus a $30 execution fee, for a total of $97. The application fee for children under sixteen is $52 plus the $30 execution fee. The passport application fee includes a $12 security surcharge, which became effective in March 2005. Pass-ports are valid for ten years. As always, check online for the most current information: http://travel.state.gov/pass-port/passport_1738.html

In the past, a driver's license or birth certificate and photo ID were sufficient for travel between the U.S. and Canada, Mexico, and many Caribbean nations. However, the Western Hemisphere Travel Initiative, which arose from the terrorist attacks of 9/11, has changed travel require-ments. Effective in January 2007, all persons traveling to the U.S. by air must present a passport or other valid travel document to enter or re-enter the country. Acceptable travel documents include Alien Registration Card, Form I-551, issued by the Department of Homeland Security to Legal Permanent Residents; Merchant Mariner Document issued by the U.S. Coast Guard; and NEXUS Air card at designated NEXUS sites (limited to citizens and residents of Canada and the U.S.). Members of the U.S. armed forces traveling on orders are exempt from the requirement to have a passport. A passport card is under development for travel within the Western Hemisphere but is not ready at this time. These restrictions are being extended to other travel to and from the U.S. by land and sea in 2008.

Many countries also require visas. A visa gives an individual permission to formally request entrance to a country during a specific period of time and for certain purposes (student, tourist, or business) and usually is stamped or glued onto a passport page; in some instances, a visa is a separate document. The U.S. State Department has a list of countries requiring U.S. citizens to have visas at: http:/ /travel.state.gov/travel/cis_pa_tw/cis/cis_1765.html

If a visa is required, you must apply via that country's U.S. embassy before departing on your trip.

Apply for your passport and a visa (if necessary) as early as possible once you decide to take a trip. Since the laws regarding passports have changed, there have been long waits for documents, and in some cases, people have missed their trips. Also, check the expiration date on your passport and current regulations. If you were over sixteen when your first passport was issued, your passport will be valid for ten years from the date. According to the U.S. State Department, "If possible, you should renew your passport approximately nine months before it expires. Some countries require that your passport be valid at least six months beyond the dates of your trip. Some airlines will not allow you to board if this requirement is not met."

If you're traveling with a child, double-check the expiration dates on his or her passport because passports expire in five years for children who received a passport when they were under the age of sixteen.

Also, if you travel often, you may need a new passport if you have run out of blank pages. Always check passport and visa regulations well in advance of your trip.

If you're cutting it close to your departure date and

you fear not getting your passport in time, official passport issuing agencies offer expedited services for a higher cost. Some online companies also promise expedited service, but be careful—make sure the company is legitimate. Some people have had success by contacting their local congressional representative to check on the status of a passport application and to help expedite the process, if possible.

Once you receive your passport, sign it immediately. It's advisable to photocopy the data page of your passport, keeping the copy separate from your passport. If you're using traveler's checks, keep the photocopy of your passport with the list of serial numbers for your checks. Likewise, leave a photocopy of the data page with the same person in the U.S. with whom you leave a list of your traveler's check serial numbers. While traveling, keep your passport and money in your "cash belt." When you reach your destination, if local laws permit, it's safest to leave your passport in a hotel safe deposit box.

If your passport is lost or stolen while you are in your destination country, report it to both the local police and the U.S. embassy or consulate immediately.

Health Concerns

If your volunteer adventure is going to take you outside the U.S., you should check any health requirements for visiting your destination country and whether there are any specific health issues. A good place to start is the website of the Centers for Disease Control and Prevention, www.cdc.gov/travel/, which provides a variety of information, including what vaccinations (if any) you will need to have before you go. If you take prescription medications, be sure to carry a copy of the original prescription (including the drug's generic name) with you at all times. For controlled substances or injectable medications, you also should have a note from your physician on letterhead.

What health-related products do you need to take with you?

Many heathcare items readily available in the U.S. are more difficult to obtain in other countries. It's recommended that travelers take a health kit with supplies to treat both pre-existing medical conditions and minor health problems that may occur during your visit. If you have allergies or diabetes, you should consider wearing an alert bracelet and be sure to have a card identifying your condition with your other travel documents.

Personal prescription medications (kept in their original containers!) and any applicable antimalarial medications should be included in the travel health kit. Also recommended by the CDC are:

- Over-the-counter antidiarrheal medication
- Antibiotic for treating moderate to severe diarrhea
- Antihistamine
- Decongestant (alone, or in combination with an antihistamine)
- Motion-sickness medication
- Over-the-counter pain or fever-relief medication (aspirin, acetaminophen, ibuprofen, etc.)
- Mild laxative
- Cough suppressant/expectorant
- Throat lozenges
- Antacid
- Antifungal and antibacterial ointments or creams
- Over-the-counter hydrocortisone cream
- Epinephrine auto-injector, especially for those with a history of severe allergic reaction (child-dosage versions are available)
- Insect-repellent (with DEET content up to 50 percent)
- SPF 15 or higher sunscreen
- Aloe gel for treating sunburn

- Digital thermometer
- Oral rehydration solution packets
- Basic first-aid supplies like adhesive bandages, gauze, ace wraps, antiseptic, tweezers, scissors, cotton-tipped applicators
- Antibacterial hand wipes or an alcohol-based hand sanitizer (at least 60 percent alcohol)
- Moleskin for blisters
- Lubricating eye drops

Depending upon your destination, other items that might come in handy include high-altitude sickness preventive medication and water purification tablets.

If you don't want to create your own travel health kit, commercial medical kits are widely available from sporting goods stores and other sources.

In the post 9/11 world, many of the liquids and sharp items in a travel health kit will have to be transported in checked luggage. However, prescription medications should always be clearly labeled, kept in their original containers, and packed in carry-on baggage.

Health Insurance

Check with your health insurance carrier to see whether it covers healthcare abroad. Medicare and Medicaid do not cover medical care outside the U.S. If your carrier does not cover international care, you should plan to obtain travel health insurance. Your insurance agent may have recommendations for such coverage. You also can find a number of companies that offer travel health insurance online.

Packing for Your Trip

You have finished your planning and learned about your destination country. You have your tickets, money (or traveler's checks), and documentation. Your departure date is nearing, and it's time to pack for your trip.

First, get a "cash belt," a wallet with a strap that will fasten around your waist under your clothes. This is where you should carry your money, tickets, and passport. Carry a small amount of cash in your wallet or purse for incidentals like snacks, tips, etc.

You can take one carry-on bag aboard the plane, plus a "personal" item like a purse, laptop computer case, or briefcase.

CARRY-ON BAG

This bag must meet airline size restrictions for fitting under a seat or into the overhead bin. It should include:

▸ Prescription medications in original, pharmacy-labeled bottles (note: if diabetic injection kits are packed, an official letter from your doctor may be required)

▸ Contacts lens supplies

▸ Hearing aids and batteries

▸ Toiletries, in containers acceptable under Transportation Security Administration restrictions; visit: www.tsa.gov and click on "For Travelers"

▸ Clothing for one or two days, in case your checked luggage is lost or misrouted

▸ Reading material and other "entertainment" items like crossword puzzles, decks of cards, CDs, etc.

▸ Jewelry

▸ Camera

▸ Snacks

▸ Comb, brush, toothbrush, and toothpaste

▸ Keys

Remember that you must stow your carry-on bag yourself, so make sure it's not too heavy for you to lift into an overhead bin.

Make sure you can easily access your toiletries, personal items, and "entertainment" items during the flight.

The simplest way to do this is to have them in your purse, computer case or briefcase, or in the outer pocket of your carry-on bag.

Checked Luggage

What clothing to pack will depend upon both your destination country's climate and social customs and what your volunteer endeavour will entail. What season will it be during your visit—do you need to pack for heat or cold? Are you going to be working in a soup kitchen or on a construction site or teaching a class? You should also factor in any personal travel or sightseeing you plan to do.

Guidebooks and websites about your destination country will provide details on the climate and acceptable dress. Remember to take into consideration where in the country you will be staying in terms of geography and population. A coastal area will differ in climate from a mountainous area and what is the norm in a major city probably differs from what is common dress in rural areas. In most instances, you will need to dress more con-servatively than you would in the U.S. This is especially true for women. In many parts of the world, shorts, short skirts, and sleeveless blouses or dresses are considered inappropriate.

Talk with your volunteer organization before decid-ing what clothes will be appropriate for your activities. Try and get the names of previous volunteers and ask them what clothes they took and what they actually found they needed during their stay—the two may not be the same.

You will want to take clothing that requires minimal care. Access to washing machines, dryers, irons, etc., may be limited. If at all possible, take clothing you can wash by hand if necessary and hang dry. Pack a small travel-size bottle of detergent if possible.

Make a list of everything you think you should pack.

Then, review it carefully. Don't take more than two or three pairs of shoes and take clothes that are multi-purpose and can be worn in layers. Most travelers will tell you they took far more than they really needed.

Ready to Go?

There is a lot to be done before you depart on your volunteer vacation, but it should be a fun beginning to your adventure. Start planning well in advance of your departure. As you can see from the information in this chapter, some of these things will take time to accomplish.

- *Learn about your destination:* Study the history and culture of your destination country, as well as the current political and social environment.
- *Get your travel documents:* Apply for your passport as early as possible and, once you receive that, any visa necessary for your destination country.
- *Make decisions about money:* Decide how you will handle your money needs—how much will you need and will you use U.S. dollars or traveler's checks?
- *Learn the language:* Learn at least enough of the local language in your destination country to communicate on a basic level.
- *Book your travel:* If your volunteer organization is not making your reservations for you, work with a travel agent or plan your trip yourself online.
- *Check health requirements:* Are any vaccinations required for your destination country? You also need to fill any needed prescriptions and assemble your travel health kit.
- *Pack your bags:* Determine what clothing you will need, make a packing list, and then trim the list as much as possible.

About the author of this chapter:

Pamela Jones is editor and director of publications for the Regulatory Affairs Professionals Society. She also volunteers in the Washington, D.C., area and has traveled to thirteen countries, many repeatedly. She lived in the Netherlands for three years and worked with volunteers in seven countries to create local professional networking organizations.

SECTION 2

Real-Life Stories

Media work in Ghana.

CHAPTER 4

Business Development

Throughout the world, the number of small and micro-businesses is growing rapidly. Volunteers can offer valuable assistance to help these community entrepreneurs on their way to economic independence. What is often needed is technical assistance and advice on matters such as business planning, budgeting, inventory systems and control, and marketing. While there are some programs, such as those run by American Jewish World Services (AJWS), that require professional experience, others do not.

As you can see from the stories below, both experienced and non-experienced business people can provide support. Laura Silver, an AJWS volunteer, applied her experience as a writer and web-content manager to assist a Kenyan organization rebrand and market itself. Schuyler Richardson assisted a small women's cooperative in Costa Rica through a Cross-Cultural Solutions program.

Laura Silver

Keur Momar Sarr is neither on most maps of Senegal, nor is it featured in the Lonely Planet's guide. Google Earth shows it as a blip in the barren sun-baked earth of the Sahel on the edge of a sprawling body of water, which I now recognize as the Lac de Guiers.

There's a lot more I know about the sandy, goat-laden town whose name means House of Momar Sarr, its first inhabitant. They are things that can't be learned from a map, a guidebook, or a passing visit to the town's Saturday market, which turns the ordinarily sleepy outpost into a cacophony of commerce, with locals from as far as fifty kilometers away buying and selling animal parts, fabrics, wash basins, and depending on the season, produce that includes mangoes, generous heads of lettuce, scallions, tomatoes, and succulent melons.

That market is the reason why I was there. Not to grow the fruits and vegetables, but to find out more about the women's groups that cultivate them and to help with the marketing and communications efforts of ASREAD, the organization that supports farming, reforestation and literacy initiatives throughout the rural region.

ASREAD, whose French name translates to the Senegalese Association for Research, Study and Support for Development, is a partner organization of the New York-

Laura Silver with Mamadou Fall, a teacher and colleague, at Keur Momar Starr's Saturday market.

Barbara Silver

based American Jewish World Service (AJWS), whose Volunteer Corps set me up with the assignment and covered the cost of my flight.

I had wanted to come to Senegal for more than a decade, inspired by writers—Mariama Bâ, Ousmane Sembène, and Léopold Sédar Senghor—whom I'd encountered in undergraduate Francophone literature classes at the University of Massachusetts. I had heard about the AJWS Volunteer Corps through a friend ten years earlier and was constantly on the verge of applying. Finally, after logging a dozen years at desk jobs in the nonprofit sector and becoming vested in my employer's pension plan, I was ready to take the plunge.

AJWS couldn't guarantee that I'd get my first choice of volunteer destination, so I prepared to go anywhere. One of the volunteer coordinators asked if I'd be okay in a rural setting. Sure, I responded, eager to take a break from the hustle-bustle of midtown Manhattan, where I'd been working as a writer and web-content manager at a major nonprofit.

It was my first trip to the African continent and, even though I was in awe of the country's literary history and enthralled by scenes of Dakar from Sembène's films, I was clueless about life in the Senegalese countryside.

Three hundred kilometers north of Dakar, on an unnamed road (paved but pocked with potholes) a sign announces Keur Momar Sarr (population 2,000–4,000, depending on whom you ask, and when). The side streets aren't strewn with sand, they are made of it—and laced with goats, kids, flattened cans, used car tires, discarded baggies, and sun-hardened animal waste. I masked my urge to make a quick getaway.

I didn't expect to have half a baguette and instant coffee for breakfast every day or to make so many new friends under the age of twelve. Faced with the clamping heat, a shortened workday, and the relaxed pace of the

African office, I didn't think we'd accomplish much, but once I settled into the local ways of doing business, I was able to get my message across and help the organization do the same.

My colleagues, all male and ten to twenty years my senior, and I generated press releases trumpeting the international cooperation at ASREAD (a pair of Portuguese volunteers were also working there) that were picked up in the Senegalese press. We started assembling a list of organizational contacts and launched a rebranding effort that included updating ASREAD's logo and painting it on signs that had faded beyond recognition. I made contacts with Senegalese journalists and wrote, edited, and designed brochures in French and English. More important, I made friends and helped ASREAD staff envision a long-term communications strategy, which includes plans for the organization's twentieth anniversary celebration in 2009.

I hope I'll be able to attend.

ASREAD staffer Daouda Ndiaye and his family share a typical lunch of tchebou djiene, fish, and rice, with Laura Silver.

Schuyler Richardson and
her son Charlie in Costa Rica.

Schuyler Richardson

In 2003, my son Charlie and I spent two weeks in Costa Rica on a Cross-Cultural Solutions program. At eighteen, he was the youngest member of the team, and I was the oldest. We were stationed in Ciudad Quesada in the middle of Costa Rica. There were a number of projects, including painting fences, working with teenage girls in a home, caring for foster children—which Charlie did. The plum job was mine: working with a group of wonderful women who had started a business making paper and tourist products like little books. They cut down banana trees, chopped up the trunks, and mixed that with recycled business paper and water in a kitchen blender. They had attended a government-run program in paper making before establishing the business with the reluctant blessings of their husbands.

I learned—if I did not know already—that women are the same all over the world and in any economic situation, our primary concern is for our children and families. These women needed to care for their families and to contribute to their families' earnings and, like so many around the globe, figured out a way to do both. Their business allowed them to work around their families' schedules and still be successful entrepreneurs.

A volunteer who had served before me was a Harvard MBA who had written a twenty-page business plan they did not fully understand. I helped on a more practical level. My biggest contribution was to set up an inventory system for the women. They did not know what they had in stock or what the prices were. I also collected payments, made a sales pitch to the rest of my team, and helped make paper and create the products. As with my American women friends, we would put on music, dance, and sing while we worked. It was a pretty great volunteer job.

What a great team I was with—a group of young people who wanted to do something for others. Each of them raised the funds for this trip and then provided hands-on care. We stayed together in one house with shared bath facilities. Since I was the oldest on the trip, I was given a private room, but that turned out to be a mixed blessing: it was directly over a bakery, and deliveries began at 4:00 a.m. Consequently, on one of our free weekends, I booked a room near Arenal Volcano with my own private bath.

After the project was completed, the whole team went to Puerto Vallarta for the weekend. There, I took on the role of mom and chaperone, suggesting that the boys (young men) and girls (young women) stay in separate hotels. Everyone stared at me blankly, and my son, who was mortified, had to explain that these young people had been staying in co-ed dormitories and group houses for years and that everyone wanted to stay together—not my college experience!

Having been on trips with two different organizations, I know that a lot depends upon both the organization's philosophy and the individual team leader. In many ways, both of my projects were led by very dedicated professionals; although we were given direction, there was not much hand-holding. One contributed what they could based on their life experiences. That was great for me. I was happy to realize how much I had to offer and to stretch myself. It was a wonderful experience.

Project in Xiloxochico, Mexico.

CHAPTER 5

Construction

The need for help with construction and infrastructure support around the globe is tremendous. As unskilled labor is incredibly valuable to an organization and a relatively easy segue into the world of volunteering for contributors, many people choose this type of project as one of their first. This was true of Bettie Peterson and her husband, who have since gone on to a number of other volunteer vacations, and for Anna Hadley, who returned from her first construction experience saying, "Anyone can do it." Other volunteers such as Barb Everhart and Coretta Bedsole have chosen to participate in construction projects after taking part in other volunteer ventures.

These opportunities exist all over the world and offer a wide variety of living situations. For example, in the stories that follow, David Taylor and his son traveled to Tanzania, Anna Hadley helped build a bridge in Thailand, Barb Everhart worked in Mexico, Maya Brodkey served in Honduras, Coretta Bedsole helped out in Ireland, and the Petersons volunteered in Costa Rica.

The Petersons

I was looking for something to do after my husband and I retired. We knew we wanted to travel and experience other cultures, and then we discovered Global Volunteers. Now, we have been on volunteer vacation trips almost every year since 1995. We were attracted by the fact that Global Volunteers is in our hometown, and we liked the organization's slogan, "Travel that feeds the soul."

Our first trip to Costa Rica was really wonderful. We had no idea what we would be doing until we arrived. Our task was building a tower in the rain forest. One of the best things about these trips is that you stretch your capabilities and do new things. This was quite an adventure. We drove a pick-up truck up the mountain daily and hauled the supplies we needed to make cement. We made the footings and hauled them up. We stayed in the home of a woman and her daughter for the two weeks we were there and were treated to wonderful, fresh food. This is just what we had sought—a way to get to know people in Costa Rica.

We have learned that Global Volunteers has ongoing projects in Santa Elena, the town we visited. Each team works on something different—renovating buildings, landscaping public spaces, painting classrooms—whatever the local project manager needs done at the time. One outstanding aspect of the Global Volunteers experience is the support by team leaders, including people in each country. Teamwork is what makes it all work, and building relationships is what it is all about. Some people ask, "Why don't you just donate some money?" The answer is that the ripple effect you see from your presence in a country, working on a local project, is immense.

Maya Brodkey

I think it started with idle Googling. I was looking for things to do after graduating from high school and typed "organic farming Latin America volunteer" or something along those lines. The second link was to the American Jewish World Service (AJWS) website. I read the description of the volunteer summer program and was sold.

Eight months later, I was stepping off an airplane in Tegucigalpa. I had signed up, along with fourteen other high school students, to spend six weeks in Honduras, building a potable water system for a rural community. The first things we saw outside the airport were chain restaurants: Pizza Hut, Burger King, KFC. Our first meal in Honduras was at Pizza Hut, a horrible American creation. *Lost,* the hit U.S. television show, was playing on the three giant plasma screens positioned around the restaurant.

We left Teguc in the morning. As enormous, busy, grimy, and crowded as the city was, it had a certain charisma. It was very colorful, very different. There were one-room tin shacks painted bright orange or neon green. Old tires were used as flowerpots, and boys were racing bicycles through traffic. Maybe that was the appeal of Honduras, the reason I loved it so much—despite the rampant poverty, the 12 percent HIV infection rate, the crime, and the stagnant economy—it was different from what I had known.

The town where we lived for five weeks, Laguna Tres, was in an isolated mountain location and had a population of about 150. It was a thirty-minute drive from Siguatepeque, the nearest city. Most of the men were farmers,

Maya Brodkey in Honduras.

growing coffee, beans, and corn on the mountains, on forty-degree slopes. In this village, only one family had a home with wooden floors. No one owned a car or even a bicycle. Most of the houses were one or two rooms, built of mud and bricks, with tarpaulins for roofs and no running water or electricity.

I had never really left the United States before, with the exception of a few trips to Mexican border towns. Before going to Honduras, my image of a developing country was a collage of barefoot women, city slums, and children with distended bellies. My experience in Honduras taught me that while, yes, those things exist, they don't make a developing country an alien universe. Despite the differences between me and the Hondurans with whom I worked and lived—language, religion, culture, and skin color—our basic wants and needs were the same. We had a common humanity: we could relate to one another, despite the differences. After work, we played soccer outside the school. We laughed when someone slipped in the mud. We shared lunch—Oreos from the Americans and plantains from the Hondurans.

The thing that most surprised me during that summer was how people reacted to us. I—a white, middle-class American—was in Honduras, one of the poorest Latin American nations. Bearing NAFTA, globalization, and the like in mind, I was expecting either resentment or confusion from the Hondurans. Instead, I was welcomed into Laguna Tres as though I were family. In the cities, strangers would stop me on the street to discuss everything from MTV to sweatshops. People seemed to be astoundingly objective; while no one was a big fan of America, they were delighted to meet individual Americans.

As selfish as it sounds, I did not go to Honduras based upon some vague desire to save the world, but because I wanted a change from my regular existence. I was tired of my regular routine and eager to see more of the world.

I did that, and I returned with a greater understanding of why I should care about people so far removed from my life. Honduras put a face on a developing country and gave me a context for words like "globalization" and "fair trade." I could see the connection between my actions and the lives of the Hondurans I met. It's impossible to create change without knowledge, without a context for that change. I came back with the realization that if I'd been born in a different country, a different skin color—if I lacked access to healthcare and education and things like *Harry Potter*—my life wouldn't be nearly as privileged, as comfortable, as it is now. And because I've had this privileged life, I have the potential, the option to create change.

Anna Hadley

I work in human resources and traveled with my boyfriend and his mother to a small Akha village in northern Thailand in the fall of 2006. In less than two weeks, we and five other Global Citizens Network (GCN) volunteers built a bridge despite the fact that none of us volunteers had any construction experience and didn't know Thai or the Akha language spoken in the village. In fact, one volunteer was visually impaired. But we made it work for everyone.

After orientation in Bangkok and Chiang Rai, including meeting officials from the local non-governmental organization that organized our project, the Mirror Art Group, we purchased our supplies (boots, buckets, rebar, sand, rock, and cement) and traveled by truck to the village of fifty families. A small stream cut through one of the village neighborhoods, and during the rainy season, it became a surging river that prevented children from going to school and adults from going to work. So our team dug holes, made concrete from the supplies, and built first the four concrete posts as support, and then the flat part of the bridge that connected the two shores of the creek.

Several knowledgeable villagers, two of whom served as translators, helped guide us in our work.

We stayed in villagers' homes—bamboo shacks above ground on stilts, with outdoor privies and solar panels installed by the government to provide light on the porches and the main living space. I changed my usual morning shower routine and opted for afternoon bathing; there was only cold water, which was tough in the morning but refreshing after a hard day's work building up a sweat.

Without any electricity, cooking was done over a fire, eggs came directly from the chicken, and meat was cooked right away. The meals were all very similar; breakfast, lunch, and dinner featured lots of white rice, some soup, green veggies, a small amount of meat, and scrambled eggs, with occasional fruit. We volunteers took turns preparing lunch for the local workers and ourselves. Breakfast and dinner were shared with our host family and now and again a random kid from another family. The village subscribed to the "whole village" theory of child rearing.

When we had finished the bridge in the village, GCN arranged travel for us that focused on the cultural immersion that is this program's hallmark. The eight of us hiked to a nearby waterfall and rode elephants. For lunch, our group visited one of our translator's village and met his family. We also traveled to Chiang Mai, the capital of the Lanna Kingdom in Thailand before taking the night train to spend a few days in Bangkok and then returned to our various U.S. destinations.

Since the trip, I think back to the people I met, our team's bridge-building accomplishments, visiting the preschool and teaching the children English by singing nursery rhymes and songs with them, and the many lifestyle differences. Mostly, I remember how satisfying the experience was, and I look forward to both additional travel in Thailand and more volunteer adventures.

Coretta Bedsole

My first volunteering experience (page 130) with Global Volunteers was so positive that I was ready to make an international trip and chose the Glencree Centre for Reconciliation, located just south of Dublin in the Wicklow Mountains. My major criteria were the schedule—I needed to go in the summer—and the fact that I had always wanted to visit Ireland.

The best thing about both experiences for me was getting to know and work with other volunteers from all over the United States. At the Glencree project, which I undertook in 2005, I made friends from all over the world. Living arrangements were double-occupancy rooms with bunk beds, and the meals served in the Centre's dining room were typical hearty Irish fare. Those affiliated with Global Volunteers attend only two weeks and work primarily on construction and beautification projects, but we also had the opportunity to meet long-term volunteers

Cora Bedsole.

George Johnson

who staff the Centre and learn about Glencree's approach to conflict resolution.

I spent mornings gardening, painting, and sanding and was also able to participate in the Centre's program activities by role-playing. One of the techniques used at Glencree is to put all the people involved in a conflict together and role play each other. My volunteer group was asked to role play some of the more common situations to give us an idea of what they do. This really brought home their message; I saw how it works.

Another positive is that Global Volunteers makes it idiot-proof. I received instructions before I left, including a packing list and special tips for living in Ireland. All the volunteers were met at the airport by our team leader and were provided with orientation that set the tone for the experience.

David Taylor
"The degree of injustice on our planet is too terrible."

My thirteen-year-old son Virgil and I spent three weeks in the North Pare mountain region of Tanzania, not far from Kilimanjaro and right on the Kenyan border. Kilomeni, the town where we lived, is, frustratingly, not on any map. Neither is the road to get there, twenty kilometers of bone-jarring driving up a washed-out climb to 5,000 feet. I must say that after driving up and down the mountain a half dozen times, we hardly noticed the road at all, especially when sandwiched into a Land Cruiser with thirteen other people piloted by an aged Franciscan friar channeling Mr. Magoo and Mario Andretti.

The area where we were is semi-arid, the main crop is sisal, and the earth is dusty and red and dotted with baobabs and acacias. In the hills, the land is exceedingly fertile and green. There are numerous *shambas* (small farms) bursting with cows, chickens, coffee, bananas, maize, vegetables, and forage for livestock. Subsistence farming is the only economic activity other than teaching school, shopkeeping, or tailoring that we encountered.

Our journey to Kilomeni was organized and arranged by the Global Citizens Network. Our project began a few years ago and involves improvements to the government primary school that serves nearly 400 students, ages five to thirteen. The project was sponsored by the Roman Catholic Diocese of the nearest market town. The nuns and priests provided room and board. Thanks to them we had some pretty excellent accommodations with running water and toilets. No one else for miles around had much in the way of plumbing. This region remarkably has had electrical service for a few years.

Our meals were taken together with the nuns and brothers. We ate a lot of rice, potatoes, spinach, *ugali* (the local staple made from maize), odd cuts of meat, and small green bananas, in every form you can imagine. Once in a

Virgil Taylor

Volunteers worked on this building—a partially abandoned primary school in Kilomeni, Tanzania.

while we had eggs. We learned to cut and chew sugar cane. We also learned to carry bricks and chop branches with a machete. The kitchen facilities were state-of-the-art, that is to say there was a stove and a sink but the stove used firewood.

Our first few days were spent wandering around in confusion. The uncertainty about the exact work to be done was due to the local community's lack of certainty about whether Americans really were going to show up and work. Nothing in Africa, especially development projects, ever goes according to plan or proceeds efficiently. When our construction project started, it was with a trip to purchase sand, cement, and rebar. GCN teams provide labor and a small amount of locally purchased supplies, sufficient only for the project at hand during the period of time each team is in the community. The community also contributes to GCN projects. In our case, the community contributed locally burnt bricks and tin for roofing, and the schoolchildren broke rocks during recess to use as aggregate in the concrete.

Site preparation consumed much of our time. Working entirely by hand, our seven-member team and the local team members cut and graded a hillside that had a seemingly endless number of great boulders buried within. Rocks were heated with burning logs until they cracked and then were split into smaller pieces. Smaller boulders were pushed and heaved with sticks and bare hands. Soil was carted off on rawhides or torn cement sacks or just tossed by hand. After a week of work, we discovered a wheelbarrow in the parish garage and this was transformative but still not a major breakthrough. It took two weeks to do what we could have accomplished in the U.S. in two days with a backhoe.

Workplace safety is not a high priority; we were lucky not to be blinded, burnt, or crushed. At least no one was badly injured, though I did get a few fingers wedged between rocks. My steel-toed boots were justifiably the envy of all the men there, most of whom were wearing flip-flops. My leather work gloves were seen as special talismans. Most of these folks never spend any time working a dirty job side by side with *mzungu* (foreigners), so just the sight of white folks covered in dirt is enough to make them come back each day. I smiled to myself at how the work resembled any school volunteer project anywhere with too many people sometimes standing around and only a few doing any real work. There was lots of gossiping, laughter, and hard work.

Despite the back-breaking work and inability to speak one another's languages, we had plenty of opportunities to meet Tanzanians. We discovered that Tanzania is a remarkably diverse and tolerant society. Midway through the construction, our entire group traveled to a nearby town, where we could be tourists, visiting the *Masai* and going

Virgil Taylor

Kilomeni primary school students greet volunteers.

shopping. We went to a *Masai* cattle market where *Masai* men of all ages were dumbfounded at our lack of interest in buying their cows. We also visited family dwellings; the *Masai* are polygamous and live in groups of huts made of plastered dung around a central corral, surrounded by animals. Virgil had the opportunity to provide art classes using his own supplies.

As visiting Americans, we were mobbed wherever we went for a few days and were often invited to people's homes. There seemed to be an endless number of ways to say hello in Swahili. It was a source of constant amusement to everyone and indicative of a culture in which greetings and salutations are very important. Virgil mastered many handshakes and phrases. I learned some slightly hip ways of greeting, which only got me in more trouble as people then launched into Swahili or Pare, and of course, I had to basically bow out of the conversation. We were always being welcomed and embraced all day, everyday. Complete strangers constantly greeted us, and both Virgil and I contrasted this with the way no one even smiles back home.

Eating out on our weekend tourist trip helped us understand the depth of the poverty there: our restaurant meal cost the equivalent of $3.50. With schoolteacher's wages being about $28 a month, it was obvious that no one we worked with, least of all the farmers, was going to have a meal out in their entire lives. Virgil noticed that the children lacked everything but the clothes they wore, which were disintegrating, and they played ball games with bundles of bound up plastic bags serving as the ball. Kids walk miles to school carrying a piece of firewood to exchange for lunch.

The poverty and chaos of African society are so completely overwhelming that to be surrounded by these issues with what seems like little opportunity to help is very distressing. Our initial instinct was to provide money to those who begged for it, but we realized that real progress and change can only be structural, locally determined, and managed. GCN strictly forbids individual gifts, which not everyone in our team respected. Ultimately Virgil and I came to realize that in fact what we were doing was our tiny, tiny piece of the solution and our gift.

We also took an opportunity when our work was completed to visit Moshi, a bustling small city with restaurants, ATMs, and Internet cafes, for a day or two before

Virgil Taylor

A schoolteacher prepares lessons at the Kilomeni Primary School in Tanzania.

heading off on safari. We had an excellent and knowledge-able game driver. I saw forty species of birds with the na-ked eye and loads of charismatic animals, including rhinos, lions, baboons, zebras, wildebeest, gazelles, and impala.

The trip was planned as a coming of age voyage for Virgil, in lieu of a more traditional Bar Mitzvah ceremony. Virgil and I traveled well together, and it will be in our minds for a lifetime. We learned to support one another and learned that in Africa, there is never a rush. We both learned some important lessons about how to live in a different culture. I am proud of my son's accomplishments; he was scrupulous and disciplined in his interactions and showed great maturity. The only Swahili word I ever used was *mwana* or son, which I said every few minutes, beam-ing, with my arm around the *mwana* himself.

One final lesson is that our culture of preposterous excess and self-absorption is disturbing; one wants to just take it all back and tell someone that the degree of injus-tice on our planet is too terrible, and that really, couldn't we just share all this wealth and all these idiotic choices with some kids who went running alongside me with ill-fitting shoes while carrying firewood to school. I hope to return to Tanzania, perhaps offering help in psychiatry, my medical specialty, and would like to make similar trips with my younger children as they approach adulthood.

Barb Everhart

After my earlier experience with Global Citizens Net-work (GCN) (page 78), I sought an opportunity to be a team leader. Therefore, my next project was as a "leader in train-ing" in Xiloxochico (pronounced Shi-lo-sho-chee-ko), in the state of Puebla in Mexico, populated by Nahuatl, who are descended from the Aztecs. My six-year-old daughter and I went with a team leader and her five-year-old daugh-ter on this week-long trip, with the intent of helping the local women's cooperative build a community center.

The trip was a fabulous experience for both me and my daughter. As a leader, I was able to gain an understanding of what it takes to plan, maintain, and execute an entire trip. This trip was scheduled to be shorter than past trips—in Mexico for one week and only four days on site in Xiloxochico. Also, the local community had just celebrated the end of the school year with fiestas that lasted the entire weekend. They were tired and unable to begin working until Monday, decreasing our time on site by another day. Because we stayed at a cooperative eco-hotel run by the Nahuatl women (which had indoor plumbing, hot water, and electricity, most of which the community members did not have), we were twenty minutes away from the site, which again, decreased our working time on site.

Barb Everhart's daughter learning to make tortillas from the Nahuat women in the village of Xiloxochico.

But the days we worked, we worked hard. Our group spent most of the first day removing building materials from the base of the building. All of the wood, nails, and bamboo were re-used as we worked with the community members to rebuild. I was amazed that there was absolutely no waste. My favorite part about rebuilding was being led some distance into the woods to cut the bamboo. The men used machetes to cut it down, and we hauled the bamboo up a hillside, through some trees, and back to the work project. The bamboo was extremely heavy, and it took two people to bring one piece to the site. The materials and equipment were primitive: the sand had to be sifted to remove the rocks, and we used wooden boxes with chicken wire for sifting. I was the worst at sand sifting,

Barb Everhart and other Global Citizens Network volunteers in the gathering room of Hotel Taselotzin, a project of the Indigenous Women's Organization.

Barb Everhart

Soccer was played after a hard day's work in Xiloxochico.

which I think was in part because I was about eighteen inches taller than the other women, so my partner and I had a hard time working together to shake our sifter.

Nevertheless, the trip was wonderful for everyone—adults and children. I was amazed at how much my daughter loved the experience. She played soccer with the other children and learned how to make tortillas. She wasn't bothered by the inequities between what she had at home and what she saw in the village. She saw people and loved them, as she always does.

Xiloxochico, Mexico.

CHAPTER 6

Cultural Preservation

Archeological digs are perhaps the most common type of cultural preservation activity open to volunteers. It was my first overseas volunteering experience, and I really learned that you did not need any knowledge or expertise to help on a dig. Just enough strength to break up, turn over, and remove dirt, in other words, "to dig." My story is below, along with that of Barb Everhart, a mother and university supervisor for student teachers in Minneapolis, Minnesota, who worked on a project through Global Citizens Network (GCN) to help maintain Native American culture in a small fishing village. Past GCN teams to this village have helped the youth build observation decks on several buildings, cleared trails, and recorded elders' stories.

Suzanne Stone

"A shovel? Why are they giving me a shovel?" I asked myself. Somehow the leaders of this dig weren't privy to my fantasy: I had envisioned myself sitting in the shade quietly and sensitively brushing centuries-old dust off pottery shards and helping re-make the jugs and plates they once had been. A shovel would be of no use in this delicate task. My next surprise was being given a pick, even less likely to be of use in my fantasy archeological dig.

But these were precisely the tools I needed and learned to use when I spent three fascinating weeks on a dig in the Galilee portion of Israel. It was the first season of a multi-year effort to excavate the bathhouse and other structures built in the area by Romans in the second century CE. My boyfriend and I had joined a team of four archeologists and about twenty other volunteers trying literally to get at the bottom of an ancient bathhouse. Earthquakes in the seventh century damaged much of the structure, and disuse from the ninth century on had covered the ruins with many feet of earth.

Every morning we were awakened at 4:30 and had to be on the bus by 5:00 a.m. We were driven from our campground on the shores of the Sea of Galilee to the site. We spent the next three hours shoveling away the top layers of dirt. While no Hebrew was necessary for this activity, I soon learned the words for "empty," "full," and "basket." About 8:30 we broke for breakfast, which was always hard boiled eggs, vegetables, and bread. Since we were working in an area where hot water contains almost 5 percent sulfur (as well as other minerals), the smell of which was always at least faintly noticeable, eggs were not always the most appetizing food that could have been provided. But they must have been in plentiful supply that spring because they often appeared on the dinner menu as well.

Lunch—the main meal—was served after an additional three to four hours of clearing away dirt, upon our return to the caravan camp. This was always a hearty and tasty meal. Nevertheless, the combination of hard, physical labor for seven hours each day and the two egg-based meals was the perfect recipe of "more movement, less food" that is the basis of any successful weight-loss diet. In fact, by the end of my three weeks, I had lost a few pounds and envisioned opening a weight-loss camp that would consist of a large dirt field, sparsely salted with fake ancient pottery shards where my clients would pay me for the privilege of back-breaking labor all day.

By our third week, we could see results of our labors, and we learned to be more careful with the shovels and axes—the floor was soon to be uncovered. And before we finished, a small corner of it was! This was very exciting, as it confirmed the archeologists' understanding of the structure and the surrounding area and gave hint of the beauty and majesty of the original building. Subsequent digs finished this initial effort. As the bathhouse was completely unearthed, Greek and Arabic inscriptions were found on plaques incorporated in the floors and walls of the bath. These provided additional information about the construction, including dedications to rulers and wealthy patrons. The bathhouse and some of the surrounding buildings—we could see the remains of an amphitheater while we were working in the bathhouse—have been restored

La Push, Washington.

Global Citizens Network

and are open to visitors. There is even a modern bath-house, with pools, Jacuzzi beds, a waterfall, and spa-type massages and treatments.

It was definitely satisfying to be part of this dig, and the satisfaction has continued over thirty years as I learned of subsequent digs, the restoration of the structures, and the establishment of a tourist spa. At the time, not being able to foresee this future, the satisfaction came in large part from the camaraderie with the other volunteers, who were mostly Europeans, and the Israeli archeologists. I learned a lot about their lives, so different from my American one, and a great deal about myself. This activity was certainly different from my ordinary life, and the "stretch" has continued to be inspirational to me. I am not afraid to try new things, go to new places, and meet new people. I know I can do things I have never done before.

Barb Everhart

I was drawn to the idea of a volunteer vacation. I was persuaded by the fact that Global Citizens Network part-ners with local grassroots organizations and meets local needs. At the time, I had two small children under the age of six, so I wanted to be a part of a short, domestic GCN trip.

In August 2005, I traveled to La Push, Washington, for one week. La Push is a fishing village on the Pacific coast of the Olympic Peninsula, and the inhabitants are primarily Quileute Native Americans. The decline of the fishing industry is one reason the people there are suffer-ing economically, but the tribe is also facing difficulties maintaining its culture. GCN partners with the tribal coun-cil and local community to help maintain the native cul-ture and language (with only three people remaining fluent) and to continue ecological projects.

Our team arrived in La Push on a Sunday and spent that day exploring the area. Throughout the trip, our en-tire team of eleven slept on the floor in one room of the elementary school building. We took turns preparing the meals that we ate together. On Monday, we attended a meeting with community and tribal members. Monday afternoon through Thursday, my team members and I worked on various projects with community members: cleaning up a burial ground with youth workers, creating a documentary video with some of the tribal elders, and clearing a hiking path from the road to the ocean.

Most of the work I personally did was creating the video, using a video recorder to capture the stories and words of the elders. Another team member, who had interviewing experience, assisted me by helping the subjects become comfortable with the taping process. At the end of our trip, like many GCN volunteers before and after us, I joined in a salmon bake and a drumming circle.

Global Citizens Network

La Push, Washington.

Building homes in Honduras.

CHAPTER 7

Disaster Relief

When disaster strikes, most people immediately ask how they can help. Our nation's outpouring of dollars, material goods, blood, and volunteer labor after every major tornado, hurricane, flood, and other natural disaster attest to our desire to help our neighbors. As the world becomes smaller, the definition of neighbor has expanded from those in our community to people all over the world. The stories below provide two examples of volunteer disaster relief. The Kahans, whose children were serving in AmeriCorps, learned about Hands On New Orleans from them and realized they could combine a trip to the Crescent City with an opportunity to help clean up the aftermath of Hurricane Katrina. Their experience was the shortest in this book—only one day—but was transformative nonetheless.

Janet McKelvey, a retired executive in Canada, traveled with other Global Crossroad volunteers to Sri Lanka to rebuild homes damaged by the devastating December 2004 tsunami. She says these two weeks were "her most rewarding and motivating personal development experience." She returned home to found TRIP Canada, a volunteer organization that is committed to helping tsunami victims through a program to rebuild homes, lives, and communities. Janet believes that the opportunity to personally deliver your donation and watch a family move into a house you helped build may be the most fulfilling and rewarding experience of a lifetime. TRIP Canada has sponsored three trips that have resulted in a village with homes, a school, and a community center.

Helene and Alan Kahan

We spent one day using some of our skills and past experiences in a totally new way and realized how much of a difference individuals can make in even small ways. We were both very impressed with Hands On New Orleans, the group with which we worked. They place volunteers in meaningful programs and make it easy for you to participate—providing training, clothing, tools, transportation, and even accommodations, if you so desire.

In the morning, we learned about the available options and immediately chose not to help in the demolition projects. You really need training for those, and since we were there such a short time, they did not seem feasible. We watched a demolition in progress while we were in the city, and it was a pretty amazing sight. The volunteers— all wearing protective gear and respirators because of concerns about mold—take a house down to the studs and clear away the debris. We were told that other teams would come to the site days later to rebuild housing. Everything with this operation needs to be well coordinated, not only with volunteer teams and their training and equipment, but also with permits from pertinent city departments.

Another option was working in a school library. This was great, really drawing on my experience as a media specialist in the county schools at home. We went to a charter school at a YMCA and spent the morning uncrating and shelving books, generally helping to organize the library. The shelves needed new identifying labels, which we made once we returned home and sent back to New Orleans. The afternoon was really fun. I went into the lower grades and read to the children—a wonderful opportunity. Alan worked in the Hands On kitchen, helping the chef prepare dinner for the seventy-five volunteers to be fed that night. Alan loves cooking and is the main chef in our home, but he does not often have the opportunity to cook on this scale. He had a great time.

Although we did not have time to do more on this trip, the experience was really fun, which was something of a surprise. We want to do it again. We learned it's fun to help other people.

Janet McKelvey

Working with a wonderful team of American and British volunteers on five houses for surviving families of the tsunami was the most amazing experience of my life. Many of us who read about the terrible circumstances faced by people living in developing countries feel that the issues are insurmountable and believe that there is little one individual can do to help. The tsunami brought all these realities into our comfortable living rooms, and thanks to the volunteer opportunity offered by Global Crossroad, I learned that one person can make a difference.

If you decide to get involved, you can get satisfaction from hard manual labor resulting in a home for a very deserving family. Getting to know and working with international volunteers and Sri Lankans is a reward in itself. The Sri Lankans are warm, gentle, caring, and generous people. Those who have almost nothing will share their homes and food with you. Should you have the opportunity to seek a family out and help them in some personal way—clothing, furnishings, a roof, job assistance—don't hesitate. For the cost of one night out in your home town, you can make a huge difference in someone's life.

For the experience to be most meaningful you need to be prepared. Working in excessive heat for six hours a day is very tough. The accommodations really are basic— shared rooms, cold showers, limited comforts—but better than how most Sri Lankans live. Our meals were fine, but you do need to get out just for some variety and a change of scenery. The tools and construction methods are rudimentary, and some days there is insufficient direction. So you need to be patient and recognize that this is likely how the work has always gotten done and, with a total of 88,767 homes and 26,179 buildings to entirely reconstruct or repair, the demand for materials must be huge.

This experience changed my life and that of many people in our group. Many of us plan to return because there is so much to do. Hopefully I will be able to convince family and friends in Toronto and the rest of Canada that this is something important to support.

Sri Lanka

i-to-i Meaningful Travel

CHAPTER 8

Environmental Work and Conservation

Environmental projects are among the most popular. Many people are drawn to working to help save endangered animals, including Muriel Horacek, Schuyler Richardson, Stephanie Kwong, Jane Stanfield, and Bettie Peterson, who traveled on projects sponsored by Earthwatch and i-to-i Meaningful Travel. Others help out by planting and maintaining gardens, as Adam Forbes did with Global Crossroad. These volunteers have had some amazing adventures, from exercising lion cubs to tracking elk, whales, and anteaters, and they have lived in a wide variety of settings. All returned from each trip enthusiastic about their projects, excited about what they had learned from scientists and other professionals, and ready to go again.

Muriel Horacek

I lived abroad for seventeen years and believed I was a seasoned world traveler, but Earthwatch has opened my eyes. In the past twelve years, I have volunteered on more than thirty-five projects all around the globe. Following my lead, my older grandchildren have each participated in four programs.

One of my favorite trips was tracking the echidna, also called the spiny anteater, in Australia. Aside from the platypus, the echnida is the only mammal that lays eggs.

The problem Earthwatch scientists were researching was the fact that no young echidna managed to survive in zoos. By tracking the animals, other Earthwatch volunteers and I learned that the babies, called puggles, nurse after they leave their mothers' pouches when they are forty-five to fifty-five days old. It was assumed that the mothers returned to nurse them every day. But the mothers return every four or five days to nurse their young until the babies are seven months old. This knowledge has enabled zoos to successfully breed and raise echnida.

We put radiotransmitters on the animals, and each of us trackers was assigned an antenna and a radio pack with a certain frequency. We listened for the animal's signal and then followed it and recorded its activities. Every so often we would pick up the animals and weigh them and perform other measurements. This was a little difficult because the animals tended to hide from the volunteers.

Another favorite was my trip to Costa Rica, where I helped monitor, measure, and track leatherback turtles. This project helped scientists learn that there are significantly fewer leatherback turtles than had been thought. The turtles visit every other year and come ashore during each nesting season. Earthwatch volunteers on this project might relocate threatened nests to the hatchery, protect hatchlings as they scramble seaward, excavate nests to determine hatching success rates, and rescue stragglers. This trip included downtime at the beach, where we could swim, tour the mangrove estuary, take a sailboat cruise, or just lie around.

I have stayed in just about every type of accommodation provided by Earthwatch, from a private room in a nice hotel in the Czech Republic to a cave in China. The accommodations are not important; I love learning what the scientists are learning and the sense of accomplishment. Where I stay and even the project in which I am involved are not the biggest draws for me; meeting and working with the project leader, the local assistants, and the other volunteers is just as rewarding as the actual research work. I have become friends with a London policeman and a New York city ballet dancer, people I would not ordinarily meet. During one trip, an archaeological dig in Peru, an assistant invited the volunteers to his baby's christening and to the all-night party that followed.

Schuyler Richardson
"Diary of a Desperate Waterford Housewife on the Earthwatch Expedition on Wildlife Trails of the American West"

Never in my life did I think that I would be excited to find an elk trail. Why? Because the trails are tamped down and easier to walk on than the sixty-degree slope covered in scree and piney loam. Out in Gibbsonville, Idaho, in ninety-something degree heat, my fourteen newfound teammates and I headed out to Sheeps Creek to map wildlife trails and measure plant cover.

I had signed up for a week near Salmon, Idaho, tracking the migratory trails of large animals like elk and moose. The animals' traditional migratory paths have been disrupted by human development and expansion, and scientists are trying to see whether the animals are following new paths that have been carved out for them. They hope these man-made "wildlife corridors" will allow the animals to continue to live in their natural territory.

I knew I was in trouble when I arrived at the airport with my matching Briggs and Riley luggage and everyone else had backpacks and duffel bags and were swapping stories of which mountains they had climbed in the last couple of years. "What" I kept asking myself over and over, "am I doing out here? Why have I gotten myself into this?"

My anxiety level started to escalate during the "safety" part of our talk the night before our first hike. Rattlesnakes, mountain lions, lack of water, twisted ankles, broken bones—all potential problems. Squeaks of fear escaped. I could barely choke down our delicious Mexican dinner at the Broken Arrow Lodge.

Okay, so I took a deep breath and prepared my backpack for the next day's activities. On our first day, Bill Newark our PI, Earthwatch talk for "Principal Investigator," taught us to identify plants that the elk would eat on their migrations—balsaroot, goat's beard, lupine, orchard grass—then on to the GPS training. This was all a bit much for me, who couldn't stop thinking about rattlesnakes and the warning hissing sounds they make before they strike. Guess I wouldn't be wearing my iPod that day! I managed to team up with Kathy, a math teacher from New Jersey, who seemed to catch on pretty fast to the GPS lecture; my survival instincts had already kicked in.

Our first day, after a two-hour hike and a delightful picnic, I was thinking, "no problem, I can do this," when I heard the feared rattlesnake hiss and practically levitated trying to get away. Not my teammates, however; they all ran to the snake to look at it and take its picture.

We started surveying the vegetation by following our individual transects and throwing down PVC pipe quadrants, estimating and recording the percentage of elk food within. (This information would later be entered into a computer.) Well, as it turned out, this particular set of transects were much longer than expected. So, Kathy and I struggled for six long hours picking our way down a very steep slope, sharing water and trail mix, laughing, crying, plodding on and on, and cheering each other along. Finally, we emerged battered and bruised. Happy to be alive, and that was the first day!

We took the next day off but continued our fieldwork for the rest of the week. I didn't know I had this in me. I'd never heard of "back country" hiking (no trails) or scree (loose rock), never worked with a GPS, or cared about different grasses. Earthwatch had stated that participants needed to be "fit for hilly country." Hilly country??? Try steep mountains. We hiked miles every day looking for hoof prints, trails, kills, and animal scat. In the evening, we returned to camp to make group dinners. Never has food tasted as good as those nights at the Broken Arrow Lodge Campground. I roomed with a teenager, Jessica, who was originally from South Africa. Not only is she brilliant, but she could also fly down those mountains like a little goat.

My last day ended with a roar, a mountain lion roar that is. I thought I was hearing things when I realized what it was and actually ran down the mountain. Ha, as though a fifty-something, overweight woman even had a chance to outrun a mountain lion.

This Earthwatch expedition was life altering on many levels. I completely left my comfort zone, and my toenails. Out there, losing toenails is humorously called "Idaho Toe" and is a very common occurrence. I met lots of new wonderful, interesting people and learned much more than I thought possible, especially in a fear-induced state.

As a postscript—I just returned from a photo safari in Tanzania and was able to observe a real-life large animal migration of zebras, wildebeests, elephants, and giraffes. I wouldn't have appreciated or understood about the importance of preserving the large animal migration routes without the Earthwatch experience. I'm already perusing the Earthwatch catalog for my next adventure and have become a believer in its statement, "Earthwatch believes that now, more than ever, we have to involve people in order to make global issues relevant and understandable, and to inspire change in communities, schools, and workplaces."

Stephanie Kwong

I first learned about i-to-i at my university and immediately wanted to join a trip working with animals. I was not able to go for a few years and then chose an easy, relatively close adventure for my first trip. "Surf and Save the Turtles," the i-to-i program I went on in the summer of 2005, was perfect for me. I love animals: I am studying biological science and zoology at university and plan on being a dog trainer. I love the outdoors, and I wanted to learn to surf.

My days were split between the surfing lessons and joining in a twenty-four-hour turtle watch. During the day, the patrol either guarded the hatcheries from poachers and predators or investigated the beach looking for turtle nests or for turtle footprints that would lead us to nests. Once we found a nest, it was added to the twenty-four-hour watch so that we could gather any newly hatched eggs and take them into our hatcheries. When pregnant, the turtles come out of the ocean and build nests. As soon as they lay their eggs, the mothers return to the water, leaving the eggs protected only by the sand they scatter over the nests.

In Costa Rica, crabs are the major predators of these eggs and the newly hatched turtles. Human poachers are also a big threat. The beach I was on was a national park, and there weren't many poachers. I didn't encounter any in my two-week stint. But I heard from other volunteers and the staff that at other sites, people need to bargain with the poachers, who support their families by selling turtle eggs.

Since sea turtles hatch at night, most of our work was done then. When the eggs hatched, we would shine a flashlight to attract the baby turtles, place them in a bucket of water, and carry them into the ocean. Normally, the hatchlings are attracted by the white of the ocean waves and automatically head toward the ocean. Of course, the trip is hazardous, as they have very little defense against their predators. Our work ensured that the turtles made it to the ocean.

We stayed in a two-story hut with an indoor cooking area. Sleeping quarters were upstairs, where we competed to be near the two open walls—makeshift windows—because it was hot at night. Even though we had been told the accommodations were at a campsite, I was surprised by the roughness of it all. And delighted. As I said, I love the outdoors and love camping, so the rougher the better for me. And most of the others on the trip were equally fine with the accommodations. We had been told that our site was outdoors, so most of us packed camping gear.

One guy, from France, had a longer adjustment period than the rest of us. There was no running water, so a makeshift shower area had been rigged up at a well. There were some walls constructed around the well to provide privacy, and you hauled up buckets of water to use as your shower. My friend and I were there, bathing in our swimsuits, when we heard this guy approaching. So we

Stephanie Kwong's first saved baby turtle.

Stephanie Kwong

Stephanie Kwong's friend, Amy, arriving at camp.

had the opportunity to demonstrate the shower. I think he was in shock at first. It took a while for him to realize that we were not kidding, and these really were our bathing facilities for the next two weeks. But he came around in a day or two.

Another part of our work was to improve the shower. Teams before us had built our shack; they lived in tents while doing so.

One of the great side benefits of the shower facilities were the howler monkeys. They hung out in the trees around the shower and would watch us bathe. They also tried to steal our clothes and towels and succeeded in liberating one woman's towel. We never saw it again. At night we could hear them howling.

The i-to-i staff provided orientation, and the local staff brought in the food and prepared our meals. Except for one night when the cook was unable to come, so I prepared food for the group. I had brought lots of packages of instant noodles, thinking I might need to augment the supplied meals, and used those along with the beans that we ate almost daily. Food was plentiful; we ate rice and beans every day, along with sausage, chicken, and fish when they were available, and plantains.

We were located on the Nicoya Peninsula with the nearest town, Samara, about an hour's walk away. We went there a few times each week to get our drinking and cooking water. That was fun. We went with wheelbarrows filled with jugs and needed to cross many rivers to get to the town. We'd have to unload the wheelbarrow to cross most of the rivers, then reload at the other end. We also used kayaks if we needed to. I loved the fact that even getting water was an adventure.

This was a great experience. I met people from all over the world who shared my loves. I really enjoyed the hands-on experience with the turtles and am looking forward to my next trip: the Lion Park in South Africa. This is so much better than volunteering at a zoo, where you never get to work directly with the animals. And the local people really appreciate what you are doing.

Stephanie Kwong (L) and the other i-to-i volunteers on their first night in Costa Rica

Ruth Dalle

Jane Stanfield with her new buddy Seddy at the Australian wallaby refuge center.

Jane Stanfield

I cried when I left the wallabies.

I just fell in love with them and with the wombat. That is always my first thought when I remember my time at the wallaby refuge center in Central Queensland, Australia. Different species of wallabies, including the bridled nailtail wallaby, are among the most endangered animals on the planet.

A few years ago, the Queensland Parks and Wildlife captured over 130 nailtails and found that they were in very poor health, suffering from malnutrition. So an Australian conservation program, Australian Animals Care and Education, decided to start a refuge where these animals could be cared for until they could be released again into the wild. The animals are bred while at the facility to help increase the population. In addition, the refuge takes in and cares for orphaned and sick kangaroos, wallabies, and wombats, as well as healthy wallabies and wombats used for a captive-breeding program, in which offspring are eventually released.

Every day for two weeks, through i-to-i Meaningful Travel, I joined two other volunteers and the family who runs the refuge in helping care for the animals, including Wiggles the Wombat. This included preparing their food, cleaning out their pens and water tanks, and helping to hold the animals when caregivers were weighing or medicating them.

Sophie Natasha Dubus

Jane Stanfield feeding Wiggles the Wombat at the Australian wallaby refuge center.

One of my main tasks was to feed the wallabies, including bottle-feeding the babies, known as joeys. The wallabies lived in large enclosures that held twelve to eighteen of them at a time. The pens were segregated by sex until breeding time. On "sweet potato night," they would all crowd together at the gate. Every other day, when they didn't receive this treat, you could just see their disappointment.

Because wallabies are nocturnal, much of this activity took place in the early morning or evenings and at night. During our free time, the volunteers helped plant trees and build fences for the facility, which was in a very rural area, in the outback, near Marlborough in Central Queensland. We also helped the staff with preparing marketing materials and grant writing. Basically, whatever skill a volunteer shows up with will be used.

I really appreciate the advice given by the i-to-i staff about this project: they are right to let potential volunteers know this is a program where you need to be flexible, prepared to work strange hours, and willing to get your hands dirty. They say, "You must have a real love of animals." And that means much more than a love of house pets. And this proved true for all the wild animal projects I worked on, three of which were through i-to-i.

Another one of my projects was working at the Eagles Nest Wildlife Hospital, also in a rural area of Australia, this time up in the northeast, near Cairns. I was joined by two other women there for four weeks. Again, a large part of our work involved feeding the animals and cleaning up their pens after they had eaten. Because of the nature of the diet of big eagles and owls—the main inhabitants at the hospital—we also took care of the animals that were eventually fed to the raptors. The mainstays of their diet are guinea pigs, rats, and mice. This did not take up a full day, so we helped in other ways: we constructed aviaries and pens for the birds. Again flexibility was a key to enjoying this program—not only in terms of the activities but also in regard to the living conditions. We were housed in trailers with porta potties.

For my third wildlife adventure with i-to-i, I traveled to another continent and lived in a suburb. For two weeks, I volunteered at the Lion Park, outside Johannesburg, South Africa. This education center specializes in the care of large predators native to Africa, including lions, leopards, cheetahs, jackals, and hyenas. Similar to zoos, the Lion Park works to educate visitors about the indigenous animal population. Unlike zoos, the Park allows visitors to pet some of the cubs in a supervised environment.

That is where the volunteers come in. We helped with rearing cubs so that they became comfortable with humans. We not only fed them and cleaned up afterwards, but also exercised the cubs by walking and playing with

Casey Straub

Jane Stanfield during feeding time at the Park in South Africa.

Jane Stanfield during nap time at the Lion Park,
outside Johannesburg, South Africa.

them. Volunteers are needed because lion cubs need feeding every few hours in their first few months. And since
this Park was one of the first to successfully breed white
lions, it is especially necessary that they have sufficient
staff to care for these rare, endangered animals.

Once again, love of animals is a necessity. Lion cubs
are quite rambunctious and even as babies, they are big. I
worked with cubs that were six months old, by which time
they were the size of large dogs. And as we were advised,
you can expect to get scratched and bitten. In fact, just
cleaning the cages was a three-person job. Two of us de-
flected the five lion cubs and one hyena cub, while the
third person did the actual cleaning. (And yes, lions and

hyenas can live together, but only as babies.) I am sure this is one of the reasons that i-to-i stressed you should be able to work in teams for this project.

Because of its location, our accommodations were a step up from my other wildlife volunteer programs. We stayed in tents, but they had electricity and beds. There also were bathroom facilities with hot showers, and a kitchen. We were taken to a nearby mall once a week for grocery shopping and prepared our own food, another reason teamwork is important.

The Park also has some giraffes, which we helped to feed. I spent as much time as possible with the giraffes. In order to feed them, you go up on a platform where you are almost eye-to-eye with these wonderful creatures.

While I was there, the staff needed help training the giraffes for filming. So we helped lure some of them into a field. A number of us would get into a jeep with six loaves of white bread. The giraffes would gallop behind us, intent on catching the bread. Whenever we stopped, all I saw were giraffe legs surrounding me, as the animals simply swarmed the jeep.

I really loved this volunteer program and the others because in each one I saw things I would never have had the opportunity to see anywhere else on earth. In each case, I got close to animals in ways I never could in any other setting.

The Petersons

Of all the volunteer trips we have taken, for sheer joy, nothing has matched the one to Hawaii with Earthwatch. My husband and I joined a team headed by two doctoral students on a whale watch. For two weeks, we just lived and breathed whales.

There were three projects. We could track whales off Lahaina in a small seventeen-foot boat and record their surface activities. Trained divers would occasionally record underwater activity with movie camera equipment. Since an adult whale weighs around 45,000 pounds, this seemed a little scary at first, but that soon faded. The excitement of seeing these magnificent mammals diving right under and around our boat was a huge high. They skillfully avoided harming us in any way.

The second project involved helping track the whales to determine how many are returning to this area each season. We would scan the horizon and with a piece of GPS equipment record spottings of whales in a designated area. We also looked at daily photographs of the flukes of whales to see if they returned from year to year. All this data that we gathered was for two staffers who were working on their theses on the migration patterns of the humpback. We helped them determine that many whales were repeaters for many years. We were trained to identify the whales and their behavior and how to record the data.

Another project while we were there had the scientists going underwater on calm days to observe and film mothers with their calves. Although we did not participate in this, we were able to view the films and learn from the scientists.

It was just great to be part of scientific discoveries. We met world-renowned experts who had done years of research. After our return, we picked up a book on whales in a local bookstore and found that the author was a man we had met on the Earthwatch trip.

We shared living quarters in a residential area with fourteen volunteers and six staff people for two weeks. We were a cross section of ages and personality types. We shared many housekeeping and custodial jobs necessary to prepare each day for our trip to the "office," the warm sunny waters of the Pacific.

In all these volunteer adventures, you can meet so many wonderful people with such interesting lives and cultures, you can't help but be changed by the experiences in a very positive way.

Adam Forbes

I participated in a Global Crossroad's agricultural project in Nepal. As tree-planting season was over soon after I arrived, there was little work to be done in the actual nursery. I saw a need for change and insisted we start new projects that directly benefited the community. The ensuing projects included plastic collection and recycling, bush and flower planting along roadsides and chowks, garden building and maintenance, farmer support, and teaching environmental awareness at local schools.

We cleaned many roadways and sorted much plastic to be recycled. The villagers were surprised yet happy to see foreigners collecting their trash. Along the way, we talked to many of them about the negatives of plastic and litter. They really seemed to be interested. Once a street or chowk was cleaned, we planted bushes. The storeowners and villagers loved them. It was a great feeling to walk down a street here and see that it was now clean.

We also helped plant and maintain a garden at the local monastery and school. It was hard work, but in both instances, the villagers and students seemed to be happy with the results and full of pride. The gardens looked great, helped the environment, and taught students about plants—all that and they were fun to make. When I left, the garden needed more flowers, which hopefully future volunteers will take care of.

The farm support was the most directly beneficial to the villagers. The farmers appreciated the seedlings we gave them, but they really needed more help. By helping to plant corn and radishes, we helped save them much time and money, and they were very grateful in the end.

Lastly, I taught in local schools, which went great! Topics covered included plastic, litter, air pollution, acid rain, and much more. The kids had fun, loved meeting us, and worked hard to think up environmental solutions. Education is so important for conservation work. I am sure in the future more volunteers will come who are interested in teaching.

Our projects helped the community and cheered up many villagers. I hope they are continued in the future.

CHAPTER 9

Healthcare

Throughout the world, agencies and organizations need volunteers who can assist with healthcare. One of the most pressing needs is for HIV/AIDS education. Two people who have provided this education share their stories: John Donegan served in Ghana with Global Crossroad, and Sara Spike in Tanzania with Global Service Corps. Both John and Sara were able to fulfill their educational missions and learn much themselves. They stayed with families in the communities they served and experienced the culture like no tourist can.

Although you don't need to be a trained healthcare provider to help out in many health-related projects, if you are a health professional, your services are highly desired. In two of ten Global Volunteer projects that Bettie Peterson and her husband have been on, she called on her nursing skills and experience.

The Petersons believe that, "Cultural exchange and friendships supercede any small contributions we make individually in two or three weeks." They also believe Margaret Mead's statement: "Never doubt that a small group of committed citizens can change the world. Indeed, it is the only thing that ever has." (Some of the Petersons' other adventures are on pages 57, 99, 112, 115, and 133.)

John Donegan

The instant the doors opened on the tarmac of Accra airport and the plane filled with the soon-to-be-typical warm-and-wet equatorial breeze, heavy with the smell of gas lamps and sweet fruit, and the sound of Ghana's beloved music—a fusion of country folk and calypso played at several decibels higher than is healthy—I knew I was finally here. Every waking moment lent itself to the makings of a great story filled with wonderful people and interesting events; often I wished that others in my life could experience this with me.

I worked with the African Hope Foundation of Ghana, which coordinates services related to the HIV/AIDS epidemic. On my first day, the wonderful project coordinator, Agnes, told me about all the great work the Foundation does: general education, support for people living with HIV/AIDS, helping children orphaned as a result of HIV/AIDS, training caregivers, and rehabilitation/prevention for street kids. The rehabilitation/prevention part mainly focuses on teaching young women practical skills such as sewing, dress-making, tie-dyeing, and catering. Learning these skills helps prevent them from entering or returning to prostitution. On graduation from the school, these women are given some financial support to set up their own businesses, and visits are then carried out to monitor their success.

I taught four days a week in this vocational school, for which I was admittedly not fully prepared, but managed with few resources! Classes were held in the upstairs of a church with a group of about twenty young women of mixed ages and abilities, but all with the most eager appetite for knowledge that I have ever encountered. I taught English, maths, some geography, history, art, and sports, but their favorite was science—anything in science. Oh, and they love singing Celine Dion songs. English is the official language in Ghana, so communicating at work was no problem.

One day a week, I also worked in the Foundation's office in central Kumasi, where they organized workshops for caregivers, support for people living with HIV/AIDS, and general sex education. I also attended a two-day seminar in Obuasi on how to be a good counselor. This was especially interesting because I got to meet the country coordinator for CARE International, which had organized the seminar. It was good to see how the whole system operates, from the few cents we donate in the West, right down to the individual community-based projects with full accountability.

Another day I participated in negotiations with the Queen Mother of a local tribe, a target group for the Foundation's education. We were trying hard to get her cooperation and permission to work with the women of the tribe on AIDS prevention education, but things are never that simple . . .

The local arrangements for my volunteer project were handled very well. At the start of my trip, I was met at the airport by Richmond, the foundation's local representative. Richmond, who is a great guy, organized everything on my trip from the transfers to the introductions, and checked up on me throughout my stay. I knew that he would help with any problem. He also showed me around the city on the weekend and took me on trips to Kumasi, the heartland of the Ashanti, and to the Ghanian Coast. But the absolute best was when Richmond led a group of the volunteers, including me, on a sightseeing trip to Mole National Park.

We traveled on a bus called "Peace and Love," best described in good humor as a hippy mini-mover, a loud rickety converted van with no windows, hard wooden seats, handrails falling from the roof, and holes in the floor revealing the road beneath. There were thirty-eight of us, plus the driver and conductor, crammed onto a twenty-two-seat bus.

On top of the bus were thirty-eight passengers' bags, six bicycles, two spare tires, a corrugated iron roof, and a goat strapped on for dear life, on occasion reminding us of its existence with a distant "maaaa" every so often. About an hour into the trip, we pulled over. A crowd ran towards us and suddenly started climbing up the sides of the bus. My thought, naturally enough, was that they must be helping those passengers who are getting off with their baggage. But nobody was getting off. The bus started up again, and we took a sharp right turn off the main road onto a dusty dirt track, with sixteen new passengers on the roof.

After spending hours along this bumpy, dusty dirt track, traveling at ten miles per hour, twenty at a good stretch, at dusk and by starlight, we eventually arrived at Mole National Park. Most of the group went straight to bed, but a few of us were determined to stay up, relax, and appreciate the place. As we sat around the pool, an elephant appeared from behind the small reception hut, blocking our view of the sign that read: "Elephants in this park are completely wild—do not approach the Elephants."

So we scrambled inside the restaurant and watched the elephant walk up and stick its trunk into the pool and spit it out again. This elephant wasn't shy, and they can attack. And no, despite what we thought, they can't be outrun (we were told this and decided to accept it rather than carry out any experiments that night). The next day we explored the park, which can only be done with an armed ranger, and lounged by the pool, the very one the elephant had been drinking out of, and hadn't since been cleaned, save for the removal of a HUGE beetle on the surface.

+   +   +

As for living arrangements, I had the privilege to become part of the Quarcoo family. The parents introduced me to the children as their new "Brother John," and I was welcomed with open arms, even though I needed a bit more energy to keep up with their soccer games and the table-tennis matches with all the neighbors! I was given my own bedroom, with a double bed, electric fan, and a delicious omelet every morning.

The food was, thankfully, not at all bad, as I had feared. Meals mostly involved fried rice or sweet potato with tomato sauce, and for dessert, oranges or pineapple. Ghanaians have a sweet tooth! A typical cup of tea will also have at least three tablespoons of sugar. My "mother" loved to introduce me to all the local foods and show me the vegetables growing in the garden. One native dish I grew to know very well is *fufu*, cassava/yam pounded into a glop. I won't miss the taste too much. My favorite meal definitely became fried plantain with ginger and freshly roasted peanuts!

On the morning of my birthday, my newfound brothers came into the room at 6 a.m. with colorful balloons with good wishes and orange juice and chocolate for breakfast! It was fantastic. In the evening, when I came back from work, the boys came in, and with great excitement insisted on leading me down by hand to their own school to meet the school director and meet all their friends.

Travel to work was via a *tro-tro*—the less than comfortable minivans that shake with the sound of music. Traffic is a nightmare, but you have to experience it like Ghanaians do. The *tro-tro* station basically involves a lot of waving, pointing, shouting, and door slamming, but the system runs remarkably well. As long as you know which queue to wait in, there's no problem. The neighbors help you figure it out. There are also "shared taxis," something between a private one and a *tro-tro*—never quite got the hang of it, involves pointing the driver in the direction you want to go and seeing if he stops!

I learned quickly that white people tend to stand out, especially when stuck in the many traffic jams. I couldn't help but feel self-conscious with people staring at me through the windows. Most people simply seemed curious, and I learned to just smile and nod. I'll never forget the experience during my first week—we were dropping off a fellow office worker at his home, when eight kids ran out of the house, jumping up and down with big, bright eyes, pointing and shouting, *"obruni, obruni"* ("white man, white man"). Thankfully I had been warned of this type of reaction in advance and reassured myself it didn't mean "attack, attack!"

People definitely stared and shouted at you, and then yelled to all their friends and neighbors to come out and look at the *obruni* walking down the street. It took a while to get used to that, but all the attention is definitely NOT threatening, just curiosity; most people will have never seen a white person up close before. Sometimes the kids asked for sweets (or a Playstation 2!), but I learned that if you say no the first time, then you won't be treated like a walking cash machine.

Ghana is different from any place I've ever been. In ways, it was a culture shock, but that is to be cherished. I met so many different people and had the chance to exchange stories and listen to people talk about their families and work with deserved pride. Of course, I also got to see the difficult side of living in the "developing world," but it is all Planet Earth, our home, and nothing but pure chance that we are born into more- or less-privileged backgrounds.

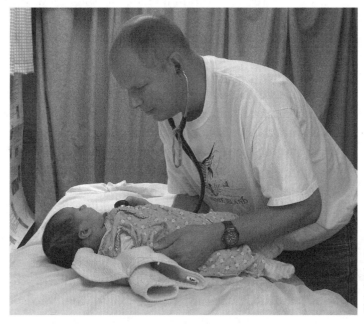

A volunteer participating in a Global Volunteers healthcare project in Ecuador.

Global Volunteers

Sara Spike
"My personal gift is teaching."

As a learning consultant with Walt Disney, I channeled my passion for teaching into a volunteer position with Global Service Corps (GSC). I worked at their HIV/AIDS Life Skills Day Camp in Arusha, Tanzania, during the summer of 2006.

My "aha" moment occurred when I first read about the global effects of HIV/AIDS in a magazine news article, which included a list of suggestions for taking action. As I believe HIV/AIDS is the challenge of our era, I saved up my vacation time and took extra personal days to participate in a long project.

My one-week orientation included lessons about the biology of HIV/AIDS, the immune system, and healthy lifestyles, and how to improve decision-making and goal-setting skills. After that week, I traveled to remote villages and lectured about HIV/AIDS prevention and treatment.

One of the biggest challenges in this instruction is respecting the local culture. I learned that many villagers practice what they call "female circumcision" and also circumcise the boys during adolescence. I had to hide my own feelings about these practices and focus on the proper sanitation methods; before my instruction, the same knife had been used repeatedly for these procedures.

Much of my instruction involved dispelling myths about HIV/AIDS transmission. The purpose of the day camps is to lessen the spread of HIV/AIDS by teaching about relationships and sexuality, as well as HIV/AIDS prevention. I learned that the young people I counseled at the day camp believed that white people and government officials could not get HIV/AIDS; they had, after all, never seen the disease affect either of these groups. In addition, they believed that an infected person could be "cured" by having sex with a virgin.

I also took advantage of my weekends to make trips to other villages, where I could meet with villagers to learn about the cultures of some of the more than 140 tribes living in Tanzania. GSC arranges these eco-tourism trips and provides a tour guide/translator. On several occasions, I discovered that the villagers did not speak Swahili, the national language of Tanzania, but only their tribal language. I learned to distinguish the different tribes by the sounds of the various languages and the clothes tribal members wore.

I lived with the most wonderful host family for the five weeks after orientation. (During orientation, I had been housed in a former boarding school.) Every evening, I stayed in and spoke with my family—a mother, father, and five children. This was an extra learning session—for both "my" family, who wanted to learn English, and me, as I learned more about Tanzania. During the day, I tried to imitate the little girls of the village by carrying water in a bucket on my head. It is very hard; the bucket is heavy and kept falling off. I paid for the water I wasted.

The fact that children have to walk to the river and carry these heavy buckets back makes it obvious what a very precious resource water is. The home had electricity service only every fourth or fifth day and no running water. On my last day, I noticed a new water spigot had been installed. I pointed to it and looked to the father of my host family. I saw a very proud man who had a tear running down his cheek expressing his joy in providing this

Global Volunteers

Volunteers help a student in a riding therapy program as part of a Global Volunteers project in Ecuador.

for his family. I know that part of the fee I paid to GSC was provided as rent to this family and made the running water possible.

I experienced many personal rewards and am now planning a return visit to Africa, hopefully teaching in the new school Oprah Winfrey has established.

The Petersons

As a retired nurse, I was pleased to go on Global Volunteer projects that focused on healthcare. One of these was to the Cook Islands, where my husband and I worked in a hospital. The facility had been closed for two years and recently reopened. Our team consisted of doctors, nurses, dieticians, therapists, and technicians, as well as nonmedical volunteers.

The hospital was very short staffed, so each of us on the team did whatever we could. Collectively, we painted a clinic, worked on nursing stations, lectured to nursing students, taught CPR, conducted home visits with their staff nurses, and helped edit nursing care plans and input them into the computer. In other words, we did whatever they asked us to do. Those without healthcare experience helped in the office.

The entire Global Volunteers team stayed in a group house with a pool. We ate there also, sharing in local cuisine, including plenty of fresh fish, taro, and coconuts. Being together facilitated team meetings, which took place every day. The local leaders and Global Volunteers' project leader made sure we received the proper orientation at the start of the project and knew what was happening every day.

The islands are incredibly beautiful. We were there for three weeks and had evenings and weekends free to explore the island. We saw some magnificent sunsets from the beaches, and we got to know a bit about the Cook Islands and its culture. The Cook Islanders celebrate life every day, wearing flowers in their hair and singing all the time. In fact, we wore garlands of fresh flowers the Islanders had woven for us on our heads as we made patient rounds—the sweet smell of tropical flowers following us everywhere.

A key word on these trips is "flexibility." Preconceived notions of project expectations can take right-hand turns at any moment. The Global Volunteers' philosophy is that when we do these projects, we consider ourselves "servant learners." We have been asked by each country to

Global Volunteers

A Global Volunteers participant helps paint a library in the Cook Islands.

help work with them on a particular project. For example, on this project, Global Volunteers partners with the Cook Islands Association of Non-Government Organizations (CIANGO).

On our way home, we visited New Zealand. These side trips, which we have made on most of our Global Volunteers trips, are a real bonus. Although we have enjoyed each place we have visited through Global Volunteers, we have never repeated a trip because there are so many other places we want to see. Our children have bought us the book, *1,000 Places to See Before You Die*, and we are trying to work our way through the list.

Another trip where my nursing experience proved valuable was to Quito, Ecuador (page 115).

CHAPTER 10

Social Services

Helping provide direct social services to the poor and needy around the globe can be both awe-inspiring and humbling. It can also be quite diverse as activities cross into such categories as direct healthcare and even construction. It is also habit-forming, as the five stories below attest.

The Petersons have taken over ten different volunteer vacations. Both Corey Stilts and Sarah Forman traveled with Cross-Cultural Solutions to Russia, where they helped take care of children and the elderly. Both were so moved by the experience that they plan to return. Similarly Chris Hanna knows she will return to Kenya, where she and her family worked in an orphanage. Gloria Gery, a retired businesswoman, has returned repeatedly to her volunteer effort at a Romanian "failure-to-thrive clinic."

These stories show the diversity of volunteers, their ages, motivations for traveling and volunteering, and their preferences for living situations and activities, as well as the type of work available. The stories also illustrate the greatest common denominator: everyone loved what they did and agreed with Chris Hanna—when you make this kind of trip, be prepared for two things: to have a life changing experience and to enjoy every single minute.

The Petersons
On our Global Volunteers trip to Ecuador, my husband and I worked in a daycare center. The facility, Fundación

Campamento Christiano Esperanza (Camp Hope), provides rehabilitation services and education for many students and custodial care for some. They also serve two good nutritional meals a day and provide medical services on a limited scale.

We helped out in various ways, including taking several of the severely handicapped students to a large indoor pool, where each student used a large inner tube with the help of a volunteer. Some of these students were young adults, and some were children. We did physical therapy and exercises with them without the luxury of warm pool water or lifts to help get them in and out of the swimming pool.

You contribute whatever you can. A civil engineer was with us on this trip, and he helped build ramps for wheelchairs so the students could be pushed from room to room. As a group, we built wooden food trays for their wheelchairs and helped with other small building projects—just pitching in however and wherever we could. I really believe that no matter what the project, you draw from your own life experiences. In addition, we all have our talents and skills, and the synergy of the group is amazing.

We went on five student home visits. Many of the handicapped students are from single-parent homes with siblings. We saw no running water or electricity, but we did see a lot of poverty. The daycare center where we worked would allow a parent to volunteer to help pay for the services provided to their children. But this was difficult as these parents needed to work at other jobs.

We saw how hard the staff works for very little pay and with very minimal equipment. It felt good to just be there and help make the daily work load a little lighter for a short while.

Our side trip from Ecuador was to the Galapagos, the renowned island off the coast of Ecuador, which offered a fantastic, unparalleled view of nature.

Corey Stilts
"Kids are kids."

With a colleague, Renee Falconer, I took a class of thirteen college students for a two-week experience in Russia in May 2006. We spent two weeks in Yaroslavl, an ancient town northeast of Moscow. Situated on the banks of the Volga and Kotorosl rivers, Yaroslavl is historically preserved, containing some of Russia's oldest architecture. It is known for its picturesque cathedrals, gold-domed churches, ancient fortresses and monasteries, as well as for its vibrant artistic community. We stayed at a hotel that is the local base for Cross-Cultural Solutions (CCS), which ensured easy access to translators and CCS staff.

We were assigned to a local hospital where we worked with children and the elderly, playing games and planning and conducting arts and crafts activities. We joined the children outside for activities and joined the older folks

Stephanie Loria

Students in front of the Church of Christ's Resurrection, in St. Petersburg.

for cards and bingo. Some of the female students also offered assistance with nail manicures. It was very gratifying to plan the activities with my students and to see how much both the givers and the receivers enjoyed the projects.

At the end of the summer, I was already planning to return: two weeks just isn't enough. It takes a week to feel comfortable, and then you start to get to know everyone. It's just too short a time. Even in a short stay, however, we all learned a lot about Russia. CCS provided programs on Russian culture, including a talk about the Russian experiences in World War II, as well as cultural immersion activities.

The orientation by the CCS staff was a big part of the success of our trip. I felt very well prepared when I left. Yet, the program itself made the trip even more successful. Even though I was prepared as far as what to bring, what my itinerary was, and what I would be doing, I was not prepared for how wonderful the country and all the people I met would be. Everyone there was extremely courteous and helpful, and the experience and the placements were terrific.

I chose this program because of the location. I grew up in the 1970s, when the former Soviet Union was our biggest enemy, and I was wondering what all the hate was about. In college and graduate school, I met some Russians and was pleasantly surprised to discover that they were nice and very interested in the United States. I also wanted to travel somewhere completely different from places I'd lived and vacationed, and wanted to continue my exploration of our former enemies. My experience with Cross-Cultural Solutions validated this. Kids are kids, no matter where you grow up. I also learned that the Russians we met are as interested in us as we are in them.

My students and I had no difficulty working with the Russian children and elderly, even though none of us spoke Russian. CCS provided a translator, plus some com-

Renee Falconer

Students at a monastery in Rostov.

munication is not dependent on oral language. The Russian children knew how to play card games such as Uno and even had the same cheating methods as their American counterparts.

Our time in Yaroslavl was a unique experience.

Sarah Forman

I had traveled quite a bit with my family and as a tourist, but wanted something different, a way to engage and interact with people in another country. Because of my ancestry, I was particularly interested in going to Russia. I searched the Internet and found the website for

Cross-Cultural Solutions, which seemed to offer the type of program I wanted.

I spent four weeks in Russia while I was in college. It was almost like a job. I spent four hours a day, five days per week at the orphanage or hospital. I planned arts and crafts activities for the kids or was simply their friend, spending time with them and talking with them (through a translator). When not working, I went about the town every day. It was surprisingly easy to meet people at the market or as I walked. Because I was interested in how my great grandparents had lived, I made a point of seeking out older people to learn about their lives in Russia. I really wanted to hear about when they were children and young adults.

The other volunteers in my group and I stayed at a tourist class hotel, which was great. I made a lot of friends among the other volunteers.

Even though I wanted to volunteer and meet people in Russia, since I had never done anything like this, I really didn't know what to expect. It turned out to be the most rewarding thing I've ever done, which is why I am saving money to go again. It also changed my life profoundly: I switched majors; I now have a double major in foreign affairs and Russian. I am planning a career in non-governmental organization work and hope to work in Russia.

Chris Hanna

I visited Kenya in August of 2005. It began as a fulfillment of my lifelong dream to visit Africa. I announced to my adult children that I had made a decision to follow my dream, and my daughter Diana volunteered to come with me. Diana has been to Africa, and I think she thought her mother needed a chaperone to help keep me out of trouble! I was overjoyed, and we immediately went to the Global Crossroad's website and filled out the applications. Now the excitement was starting to grow! Global Crossroad was wonderful in answering my numerous questions. The staff was always patient and kind and available to provide any information. They made me feel that I had made the right decision in choosing them as the company to assist me in my plans.

We started reading tour books, surfing the Internet, and getting reports from other people who had volunteered to increase our knowledge of the people and culture of Kenya. We got all of our required shots for travel, passports and visas, plane tickets, and cameras and really thought we were well prepared for our adventure. But little did I know that there is nothing that will prepare you for what you will experience. I thought I would be going to help children, learn about a different culture, and see a beautiful country—not in my wildest dreams did I think that it would teach me more about myself and give me a deep appreciation of the country that I live in.

We arrived in Nairobi late at night and with the help of some very nice people in the airport got a safe taxi and went to the hotel we had previously booked. Early the next morning, our program coordinator met us in the hotel lobby. Just seeing Beckie and her smiling face put me at ease. We were immediately taken to our host family's home and were greeted warmly by Susan, our host mother. She became our rock! Susan, her husband John, and her beautiful sons made us feel right at home. The food was terrific, the conversation wonderful, and we developed a close relationship with our family. Susan gently guided us, answered questions, and took excellent care of us while we were in their home. She truly cared that we were comfortable and safe and that we felt welcomed. English is the second language of many of the people there so communication is not a problem.

After dropping off our luggage, we were taken to the ByGrace Orphanage. I am a nurse and have worked in poverty areas and thought I knew what to expect. I had read about developing countries and believed I knew what being poor meant—and then we entered the slum district where the orphanage is located. I was speechless. The smells, noise, confusion, and dirt were shocking. My excitement quickly turned to horror as I first looked at the orphanage. And then my horror turned to joy when I saw the smiling faces of the children and the welcoming greetings from the staff and headmaster. They were all so happy to see us! They made us forget the initial shock and made us feel like we were the most important people in the world!

Salome, the administrator, is a woman dedicating her life to helping the street children live healthy, happy lives. Salome is happy to answer questions and explain the ways of the orphanage. While working with her, I learned that you must enter these opportunities with an open mind and heart: don't judge the way things are done, but do ask questions when you don't understand something. Remember that you are in a different culture and that what we see as priorities are not always priorities there. An example: money must go to food for the children first and only then are extras—like schoolbooks—purchased. There are more than 160 children at ByGrace, and at times providing one meal a day for them is a mighty feat.

If you take a trip like this, be prepared to be shocked at the bathroom facilities, lack of personal hygiene products, and seeing fifteen children sleeping in one room on thin mats. Be prepared to cry when you hear the personal stories of the children. Some have been found alone on the streets; others have lost both parents to HIV. And the abuse they have endured from neighbors or family members will make you realize how very lucky you are and how very lucky they are to have found this refuge. And through all this, they smile, sing, and tell you how thankful they are to be at the center because it is a million times better than the streets they have come from. The children, age three through teenagers, are healthy, polite, and happy.

They are being well educated. Although they share textbooks, they are well spoken and can communicate on many subjects from world events to biology. They love to hear about life in other countries and to discuss what they plan on doing as adults. They will absolutely steal your heart. They have little in personal effects but are thankful for the smallest thing like an orange or your smile or hug. The orphanage may be physically lacking, but it has made many changes, and each new improvement is considered a blessing and a reason to celebrate. Each child, teacher, and volunteer will make you feel welcomed and appreciated.

We had a lot of fun, too. We brought balloons and held a parade in the play yard. There is also a lot of singing, joking, and volleyball and soccer. All they want is your attention, and they give back so much love. After the first day, you no longer see the dismal surroundings; you see only the smiling faces of the children and feel the warmth of their excitement just seeing you walk in the door.

I loved my adventure in Africa, and believe me, it was a trip of a lifetime. Our experience included a safari. We saw hundreds of animals and incredible scenery, ate great food, and met many people from other countries. We all had a wonderful time trading stories. I learned so much, and though I helped others, the experience gave ME back so much more! I was filled with the joy of helping people, and at the same time, I learned so much about myself and now truly appreciate what I have. I have begun to understand how difficult living in a developing country is and the obstacles these people face. They work hard but fight against government corruption and neglect, small salaries, and few modern conveniences. (I felt like kissing my microwave and refrigerator when I returned home.)

I met people who give everything to others even though they have very little themselves, people with so much courage and strength that they became heroes in my heart.

Some tips for others planning a trip to Kenya:

- Prepare yourself for the number of beggars on the streets and hold your wallet tight.
- If you decide to go to the Masai Market, go with a local person and not alone.
- Bring a fanny pack or small backpack for carrying essentials like antiseptic wipes, money, camera, etc.
- There are many Internet cafes, although they are very slow and not always available. It sometimes takes ten minutes to send one e-mail. So let your family know ahead that this may be a problem, especially if it is your only way of communication.
- Bring extra money to use on your weekend trips and for shopping.
- The electricity in Kenya is very unstable so bring things with you that can be done with a flashlight like cards, crossword puzzles, etc.
- You may want to bring something from your state or country for gifts to your host family.
- Also remember to bring your sense of humor and go with the understanding that nothing is done quickly in Africa.
- Prepare yourself for a life-changing experience and enjoy every single minute!

I left my heart there and will return.

Gloria Gery
"I never feel so important as when I'm there."

I was always attracted to various "do good" projects, and my husband was going on a two-week vacation. So, when I read about Global Volunteers in *Business Week*, I said "why not?" and immediately signed up and went to Romania in December 2004 for the first of my four volunteer vacations.

I was attracted to Global Volunteers, in part, because the volunteers are housed in a hotel (which turned out to be fine, clean, and very safe). I wanted to be able to be alone in the evening if I was tired from the day's activities. It was a pleasant surprise on my first visit to find that conditions were not as bad as I had expected, but I was still surprised at how difficult things were. The food was okay, but I ordered my food grilled because otherwise it was too greasy, and you have to order things like an apple a day ahead.

We volunteers ate in a room by ourselves in the non-smoking dining room since the regular dining room was very smoke-filled. Second-hand smoke is the biggest health risk here to volunteers, and the tap water is not safe to drink.

On my first trip, I immediately took a sightseeing tour of Bucharest before traveling to Barlad, where I volunteered. The car was an old Romanian model, with a seat that was halfway down, requiring me to hold onto the side to sit up straight and see. I was struck by the odd and not very attractive blend of Communist concrete block buildings and old French baroque buildings. Since that first visit, I have seen vast improvement in the country's infrastructure: lights are on, stores have merchandise, and there are more cars.

On each trip, I worked at a "failure-to-thrive clinic," where I helped care for children from a few months of age to three years old. Most children are abandoned and others simply in need of greater care than they could receive at home. The hospital focuses on nutritional needs. There are also special needs kids who require additional medical care. The work consists of caring for the children—bathing, dressing, and helping to feed them—and simply holding and playing with them, actions that help the children to thrive. In my first trip journal, I wrote, "I have never been clung to so much in my life."

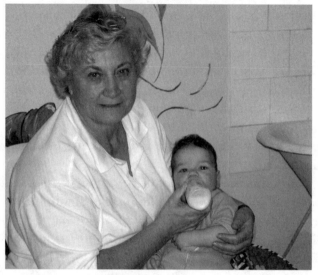

Robert Gery

*Gloria Gery with one of the infants
she has cared for in Romania.*

I was also surprised by "instant engagement." Despite the fact that I speak no Romanian, I have connected on an emotional level with these children (seeing some of them again on later trips), with my team leader (we have a reunion every time I return to Romania), with the staff with whom I work, and with the staff from my hotel. I feel very connected to these people, and we hug one another each time we meet. I know these women support their families. I respect that, and I respect their efforts with the children. I did not expect the children to be as healthy and as joyous as they are. I also have made lasting friendships with other volunteers, people I would never have met otherwise—people from all different lifestyles, careers, and interests. All the volunteers share common goals even though our ages range from sixteen to seventy-one. It makes it all the more interesting and we laugh a lot.

The biggest surprise to me was the profound and fundamental change I experienced during my first trip that continues to be reinforced with each return visit: I realized how little all the stuff I surround myself with matters and am disgusted by the preoccupation with material things I now see when I return to the U.S. Of course, I continue to buy what I need, but I find that I examine things differently.

My philosophy has become "learn, earn, return." As a result of my experiences, I feel like a bead in a continuous chain of volunteers whose commitment and work matters collectively. I always wanted to make a difference in the world and now I believe that I have.

Gloria and Bob Gery, volunteers in Romania.

Marsha Seidman

Teaching in Kenya.

i-to-i Meaningful Travel

Chapter 11

Teaching

Teaching is one of the best ways to get to know the people of another culture or land. The four stories of these volunteer vacations show the breadth of teaching experiences awaiting you. Kelly Ferguson, a college student, went to Kenya with i-to-i Meaningful Travel and taught art, physical education, geography, and history, as well as English to grade schoolers. The others who tell their stories below all taught English, but in a variety of countries and settings and to very different groups.

On her first Global Volunteers trip, Coretta Bedsole stuck close to home and taught English as a second language in Minnesota. The Petersons taught conversational English at the college level in Mexico and China, both with Global Volunteers (GV). The Petersons remember that with Global Volunteers, each day one person shares a thought for the day in the group's journal. Some of the more memorable thoughts, especially apt for their teaching experiences, include:

- "When traveling abroad, look not back at your home shores. Leave your prejudice at the last port of call." (Thales of Miletus)
- "The greater danger for most of us is not that our reach is too high and we miss it, but that it is too low and we achieve it." (Michelangelo)

▸ "You make a living by what you get; you make a life by what you give." (Winston Churchill)

Coretta Bedsole

Coretta Bedsole, a contract lobbyist and owner of Progressive Lobbying Solutions, thanks the fact she had the flu and the Oprah show she watched that day for her volunteering experiences.

Global Volunteers was highlighted on the show, and I just felt fortunate and blessed and wanted to start making a difference. My first volunteer vacation was one week in August 2003 at Pelican Rapids, Minnesota, where I taught English as a second language. Global Volunteers runs an English language summer camp for children who live in homes where English is either not spoken at all or spoken very little. This camp helps the children sharpen their English skills before they return to school in the fall. The days are filled with camp activities including games, stories, and arts and crafts, all conducted in English.

Kelly Ferguson

As a student in the Bachelor of Arts/Bachelor of Education concurrent program at Queen's University, I was looking for practical teaching experience outside of Canada. As a result, I went to Mombasa, Kenya, in the summer of 2006 with i-to-i Meaningful Travel.

Although I'm not sure why, I had always wanted to go to Kenya, so I searched the Internet for teaching experiences there. The support promised by i-to-i was very appealing, which is one of the reasons I chose that program.

Whatever I was looking for in Kenya, I found it. It was by far one of the most enriching experiences of my life, and I learned more from this trip than I could ever have hoped. The possibility of seeing wildlife really appealed to me, and as it turned out, going on a safari during my free time was one of the highlights of the trip. Though the safari

Kelly Ferguson

*Kelly Ferguson surrounded by some of her new friends
from Living World Primary School in Mikindani, Kenya.*

and other weekend trips were certainly amazing, I enjoyed
the volunteer experience so much that I tried to avoid taking too much time off for outside excursions.

My project lasted six weeks. I expected to teach English to nine- to twelve-year-olds, but found that I taught
much more, including art, physical education, geography,
and history. Both Kiswahili and English are spoken and
taught in Kenya. All of the classes I taught were conducted
in English, and most of the students I worked with had
some knowledge of the English language.

My teaching experience in Kenya was different from
my Canadian teaching experience, and in that sense, had
many challenges and rewards. Education in Kenya is more
traditional, with teachers lecturing most of the day rather
than the group work and interactive education we are

accustomed to in Canada. I gained valuable experience in managing a classroom and approaching unfamiliar curriculum content, especially with the help of the trained staff at the school. It was gratifying that the Kenyan teachers also appreciated my input; they saw some new ways to do things and learned about new art projects from me. Once I get my degree, I will stick with my original career plan and begin teaching in Canada, but now I know there are other options in the future.

The support i-to-i promised proved to be real. There were about twenty-five volunteers in the area every week I was there; three of us were at my school. We all met every Wednesday with two in-team coordinators from Kenya and one woman from the United Kingdom. This was a valuable part of the program; it was nice to know there were people I could call if I needed them. I liked having a foundation to

Taking a break from schoolwork to take a class photo.

Kelly Ferguson

support me if it was needed. In fact, one of the volunteers became ill during her stay and called the coordinators, who came and took her to the doctor immediately.

Another volunteer and I stayed in the home of a young family with two small boys. This was a wonderful part of the program; the family members were terrific hosts and provided our meals. I also enjoyed meeting and getting to know the other volunteers staying in the area, mostly people my age from the U.S. and U.K. Given our interests, it was almost guaranteed we would form friendships right from the start.

I'm not sure what I was expecting except a great experience—and my expectations certainly were fulfilled. I loved finding how much was the same: the kids in the classroom were excited to be learning, bouncing in their seats with raised hands, just like the kids I've worked with back in Canada.

One of the best parts of the trip was immersing myself in the culture in a way that is not possible as a tourist. I formed relationships with people there and felt as though I became part of the country. Tourists meet only a limited number of people and often in just a few settings, whereas I was living and working among Kenyans, a much richer experience.

I have so many good memories of my trip, but I also remember sometimes feeling helpless while I was there. The need is great, and the limitations on what you can do are frustrating. I am now sponsoring one of the children from the school where I taught, after asking the headmistress to recommend someone. In this way I will be able to keep a small connection to all of the wonderful people I met during my time in Mombasa, Kenya.

The Petersons
Our trips with Global Volunteers have transformed our lives. We read more now and are much more tolerant

of other people and appreciative of their cultures. We also have done things we never dreamed we would do. For my husband, that includes working with handicapped children. For me, it was teaching. Two of our trips have involved teaching conversational English. One was a three-week trip to China, where we taught seventy students at the university level. Since I had never taught before, I was scared to death, although I am very comfortable with one-on-one interactions. Now, I am very proud that I did it. I have learned you can do more than you think possible.

There was no curriculum, so I had to plan the whole course. In the morning class, I read from a book that the students had. It was about American families and how they interacted with each other. I read out loud, one sentence at a time, which the students would then repeat after me. With a class of about seventy students, this worked pretty well. It was easy to hear which words were giving them the most trouble. I would write the word on the chalkboard so they could read it. Then we would repeat it a few times together. I would then focus on words they had missed.

The afternoon class was smaller and the students in it had better English skills. Many of these students were hoping to get jobs with joint-venture companies and needed to read, write, and converse in English. We held conversations about whatever the students wanted to learn. One thing that helped was that I had just completed ten years as a college student, so I drew on my own experiences. The students were very respectful, which also helped a great deal.

This trip offered some unique opportunities for interacting with the Chinese people. One evening, my husband and I visited a student's home where she lived with four generations of her family, including a great grandmother. We were warmly received and prepared a meal together—it included soup, pork, and some homemade dumplings. It was delicious. Then we spent the evening sharing our cultures and toasting to each other with wheat wine. We toasted family, friends, country. We toasted to returning and them coming to America some day.

Our Chinese Global Volunteer host took us to many wonderful places. We saw the Terra Cotta Warrior archeological site. We walked the Wall surrounding Xian City, where we were stationed. We visited a Taoist Temple and had the rare opportunity to listen to a young Chinese man tell us of his journey. He said they travel from master to master to learn about the martial arts, herbal medicines, and meditation. Our host interpreted his Chinese for us.

Our other teaching experience was in a college in Queretaro, Mexico. While this was also at the college level, it was very different from the situation in China. This time, we worked with the teachers in the classrooms. Each teacher had a different agenda as some were in test week and needed to stick to certain criteria. In any case, we introduced ourselves to the class, giving them some of our background. Students would ask us questions in English, and we would answer them in English. The Mexican students, like the Chinese, had studied English before college, but they had had little opportunity to speak it. What they needed most was to hear the language spoken and develop an ear for the various sounds. Some students would come to us for one-on-one time to practice their English.

In Mexico, we had some documents stolen, including our passports. Our team leader called one of the larger hotels and got us a driver for the next day. She also scheduled an appointment for us with the American embassy in Mexico City. She and my husband and I spent much of the next day traveling and eventually procuring temporary passports, which we got that same day. This was a huge learning experience for us, and eventually we were able to get reimbursed for our other stolen goods. We learned to have two forms of identification and copies of all our important documents, and to keep good records of everything.

Our team leader said, "Most problems in travel are just inconveniences." She added, "Ask for things from others sounding like you expect to get it." Sage advice, I thought.

On both these trips our teams stayed in hotels. In China, we were on the twentieth floor, and every morning we would look outside and see a sea of people practicing Tai Chi. In Mexico, we were in a family-owned hotel, which added to our ability to get to know the Mexican people.

SECTION 3

Sources

Tanzanian child.

Virgil Taylor

ORGANIZATIONS

American Jewish World Service
Headquarters: New York
45 West 36th Street
New York, NY 10018
Tel: 212-792-2900 or toll free 800-889-7146
Fax: 212-792-2930

San Francisco, CA
131 Steuart Street, Suite 200
San Francisco, CA 94105
Tel: 415-593-3280

Washington, DC
1413 K Street NW, 5th Floor
Washington, DC 20005
Tel: 202-408-1380

www.ajws.org
ajws@ajws.org

ABOUT

American Jewish World Service (AJWS) is an international development organization dedicated to alleviating poverty, hunger, and disease. Founded in 1985, AJWS first began sending volunteers into the field in 1994. Since then, more than 2,000 people have participated in AJWS programs. AJWS offers numerous opportunities for high-school-aged and college-aged young adults and adult professionals to volunteer in Africa, Asia, or the Americas.

TIME REQUIREMENT

High school-aged and college-aged participants can participate in AJWS Volunteer Summer, which lasts for seven weeks, or AJWS Alternative Breaks, which lasts for one week to ten days. Young adults and adult professionals can participate in AJWS World Partners Fellowship or Volunteer Corps, with placements ranging in length from two months to one year, the average being three to four months.

AJWS VOLUNTEER SUMMER

AJWS offers seven-week summer projects for young adults between the ages of sixteen and twenty-four. These projects, which require intense physical labor approximately seven hours a day, five days a week, include structured discussions at least four times a week and opportunities for cross-cultural exchange and community building. For the next ten months, participants join retreats, write articles, speak about their experiences, and continue to provide volunteer service. These volunteer groups consist of fifteen participants and two or three AJWS leaders.

AJWS ALTERNATIVE BREAKS

AJWS offers weeklong programs to college students. In partnership with AJWS, local grassroots NGOs in developing countries invite students to participate in their work. Ten to fifteen students join one or two leaders on these programs.

AJWS WORLD PARTNERS FELLOWSHIP

The WPF is awarded to Jewish recent college graduates and young professionals who wish to volunteer at an NGO, live independently in a developing country, and participate in a peer-learning community. Fellows learn about human rights in an international context, explore values that motivate their work, and gain skills to prepare their entrance into careers dedicated to social justice.

AJWS VOLUNTEER CORPS

AJWS Volunteer Corps places professional Jewish women and men on volunteer assignments with local NGOs in developing countries. Volunteers come from a variety of backgrounds and provide skills training, technical consultancy, and general support.

FOREIGN LANGUAGE REQUIREMENT

All assignments only require English skills, with the exception of placements in the Americas, where fluency in Spanish is required, and some placements in francophone Africa.

EXPERIENCE OR SKILLS NEEDED

For programs open to adults, AJWS requires professional skills in one or more of the following areas: organizational development, fundraising, finance and administration, communications/public relations, computer technology, small business, social work, healthcare, mental health, public health and HIV/AIDS, education, law and advocacy, community organizing, and administrative support. AJWS also recommends that only people who are comfortable traveling or living on their own in the developing world and working in an environment with a high level of ambiguity and uncertainty be considered for placement.

No professional skill or prior experience is required for summer or alternative breaks projects for young adults.

AGES

The minimum age for AJWS volunteer opportunities varies depending on the program. There are volunteer placements available for young adults (high school- and college-aged) as well as adults (from young professionals to senior citizens).

COUNTRIES

Cambodia, El Salvador, Dominican Republic, Ghana, Guatemala, Honduras, India, Mexico, Nicaragua, Peru, Senegal, South Africa, Thailand, Uganda.

AJWS staff takes volunteers' preferences into consideration in the placement process, but placements are also made based upon NGO partners' needs. Volunteers are asked to be as flexible as possible regarding location.

ACTIVITIES

- ‣ Economic development—providing training and resources to individuals and families, establishing access to microfinance savings and credit for borrowers, and intensive training in financial and small business management skills.
- ‣ Education projects—promoting education in underserved communities, engaging women and girls, and providing access to learning.
- ‣ Health education—training and supporting local health workers.
- ‣ HIV/AIDs—supporting local groups that are devising effective and innovative strategies to limit the

spread and mitigate the effects of HIV/AIDS in their communities.

▸ Sustainable agriculture—increasing food security, crop diversification, and the protection of natural resources in projects that provide vital technical and material resources for improving nutrition and increasing income generation.

▸ Women empowerment—supporting programs and projects designed to empower women to transform their own lives and make lasting and meaningful change for themselves, their families, and their communities.

Cost

AJWS Volunteer Summer and AJWS Alternative Breaks both carry fees, which are highly subsidized by AJWS. The program fees cover all costs of food, lodging while in the field, tools, and supplies for the group's work project, basic staff costs, and financial support for the host organization in their primary work. These fees do not include airfare, inoculations/medications, or entry and exit taxes.

No fee is required to participate in the AJWS Volunteer Corps. AJWS pays volunteers' airfares and provides emergency evacuation assistance and medical referrals through International SOS. Volunteers are financially responsible for health insurance and in-country living expenses, including housing, food, and local transportation. These costs vary based upon the location. Volunteers can apply for AJWS funding to help cover room and board.

Accommodations

AJWS asks NGOs to assist volunteers in locating and securing housing. Volunteer Summer and Alternative Breaks participants stay in group housing provided by their host community. World Partners and Volunteer Corps participants usually stay in rented apartments that are secured upon their arrival.

ORIENTATION

AJWS New York-based staff and AJWS country representatives are in constant contact with volunteers throughout their placements.

APPLICATION PROCESS

Applications for Spring/Winter placement are accepted in late summer.

AJWS volunteer stories can be found on pages 49 and 58 (Laura Silver and Maya Brodkey).

Cross-Cultural Solutions

2 Clinton Place
New Rochelle, NY 10801
Tel: 800-380-4777
Fax: 914-632-8494

www.crossculturalsolutions.org
info@crossculturalsolutions.org

ABOUT

Cross-Cultural Solutions (CCS) works to provide volunteers for local organizations called "Partner Programs" in twelve countries. Each site undergoes an annual performance review to ensure program quality, overall volunteer satisfaction, adherence to staff policies, medical procedure training, and security guidelines.

Its philosophy is that "the most successful approach to international volunteering is one that defers to the needs and goals of the local community." It provides experienced, local, in-country staff and offers opportunities to "volunteer side-by-side with local people and experience another culture." The CCS experience also includes learning activities and educating volunteers about the local culture.

CCS was founded in 1995 and has more than 10,000

alumni. It has a worldwide staff of more than 250 people in twelve countries, with administrative offices also in the United States, United Kingdom, Canada, and Australia. In the U.S., CCS is a nonprofit 501(c)(3) organization. In the U.K., it is a Registered Charity and a Registered Company Limited by Guarantee.

TIME REQUIREMENT
One to twelve weeks (three-week minimum stays in Ghana, India, Morocco, South Africa, and Tanzania).

LANGUAGE REQUIREMENT
None.

EXPERIENCE OR SKILLS NEEDED
No prior experience or skills are required, although healthcare placements can draw on professional healthcare experience, and custom placements may be possible for certain professionals.

AGES
Minimum age is eighteen years when unaccompanied by an adult (although in some programs, sixteen- and seventeen-year-olds are accepted at the discretion of the Program Manager). Minimum age for a child traveling with a parent or guardian is eight years old. If a volunteer is between the ages of eight and sixteen, the accompanying adult must be a parent, legal guardian, or person appointed by that parent or guardian.

Also offers "Intern Abroad" programs for students seeking academic credit, international work experience, or field research.

COUNTRIES
Brazil, China, Costa Rica, Ghana, Guatemala, India, Morocco, Peru, Russia, South Africa, Tanzania, Thailand.

ACTIVITIES

▸ Infant and childcare—helping feed, clothe, and care for children in institutions.

▸ Teaching (educational games, arts and crafts, sports) and serving as teacher's aide (in such subjects as science, music, sports, and drama).

▸ Teaching English.

▸ Caring for the elderly—leading singing and dancing programs, running exercise activities, playing games, developing arts and crafts projects, preparing meals, and feeding.

▸ Working with the disabled— providing nutrition, education, and healthcare; teaching life skills; assisting with daily routines such as feeding and cleaning; and assisting with physical therapy, recreational activities, music, and exercise.

▸ Healthcare—changing bandages, taking blood pressure, weighing babies, and providing education about basic health and nutrition; more experienced volunteers may shadow health practitioners and exchange ideas and experiences; this can also include working with people affected by HIV/AIDS.

▸ Volunteer programs are conducted in orphanages and childcare centers, schools, health clinics and hospitals, homes for the elderly, centers for people with disabilities, and other community organizations.

COST

At time of publication, the base fee for two weeks is $2,489; each additional week is $272. This fee includes lodging, meals, travel medical insurance, ground transportation, in-country orientation and educational programs, language assistance, professional locally based staff, informational documents, local phone calls, incoming international phone service, and a toll-free emergency hotline in the United States. CCS advises that program fees are 100 percent tax-deductible for U.S. residents. In addition, many people successfully fundraise their fees. Contributions made to Cross-Cultural Solutions may be tax-deductible; please consult your tax advisor.

Airfare is not included.

ACCOMMODATIONS

Typical housing consists of a comfortable house in a safe, conveniently located neighborhood. Clean, modest accommodations with shared occupancy rooms are the standard. Lodging arrangements always have basic amenities like linens and running water. Local cooks prepare and serve daily meals and snacks based on the regional cuisine.

FREE TIME

Free time is available some afternoons, most evenings, and every weekend. The local staff can suggest places to visit.

ORIENTATION

In-country staff gives in-country orientation. In addition, handbooks are sent to all volunteers with valuable information about the specific country. Once the volunteer receives the handbook, Program Managers answer all questions and provide one-on-one guidance.

APPLICATION PROCESS

Need to enroll at least sixty days before the start date of the program in which you plan to participate.

CCS volunteer stories can be found on pages 53, 116, and 119 (Schuyler Richardson, Corey Stilts, and Sarah Forman).

Earthwatch

3 Clocktower Place, Suite 100
Box 75
Maynard, MA 01754-0075
Tel: 800-776-0188
Fax 978-461-2332

www.earthwatch.org
info@earthwatch.org

ABOUT

Earthwatch Institute is an international nonprofit organization that supports scientific field research and offers volunteers the opportunity to join research teams around the world. Approximately 4,000 people volunteer every year in 130 to 140 field research projects. The teams—generally consisting of four to fifteen people—are diverse in experience, age and nationality, with about one-third of each team consisting of repeat volunteers. Each project is led by a researcher known as the Principal Investigators (PI).

Earthwatch believes that teaching and promoting scientific literacy is the best systematic approach and solution to the many complex environmental and social issues facing society today. Its mission is to promote the understanding and action necessary for a sustainable environment.

Founded in 1971, Earthwatch has a staff of more than 150, with headquarters in Maynard, Massachusetts, and offices in Oxford, England; Melbourne, Australia; and Tokyo, Japan. It is a public charity described under Section 501(c)(3) of the U.S. Internal Revenue Code.

TIME REQUIREMENT

Nine to twenty-one days.

FOREIGN LANGUAGE REQUIREMENT

The primary language spoken on all Earthwatch projects is English, so no special language skills are required. On some projects, however, language skills—although not necessary—can be a great help to the researcher.

EXPERIENCE OR SKILLS NEEDED

Generally, no special skills or experience are necessary, although some projects may require scuba qualifications or high fitness levels.

AGES

The minimum age is eighteen years when unaccompanied by a parent or guardian; with a parent or guardian, the minimum age is sixteen. Teen teams are exclusively for sixteen- and seventeen-year-olds, and are supervised by additional Earthwatch staff. Earthwatch also offers group expeditions for educational and community groups (e.g., environmental organizations, religious institutions, book clubs, sports teams, alumni associations, or simply groups of friends) and family teams, which have a minimum age of ten or thirteen, depending upon the expedition. Discounts are available for group trips.

COUNTRIES

Arctic, Argentina, Australia, Bahamas, Belarus, Belize, Bohemia, Botswana, Brazil, Cameroon, Canada, China, Costa Rica, Easter Islands, Ecuador, England, Greece, Iceland, Japan, Kenya, Madagascar, Malaysia, Mexico, Namibia, New Zealand, Peru, Puerto Rico, Portugal, Romania, Russia, Seychelles, South Africa, Spain, Sri Lanka, Thailand, U.S. (Alaska, Arizona, California, New Jersey), Vietnam.

ACTIVITIES

The research supported by Earthwatch includes:

> Environmental impacts—how human activities affect ecosystems, endangered habitats, and threatened species.

> Biodiversity—how ecological and cultural forces relate to ecosystem processes that maintain biological diversity.

> Human ecology—how the environment shapes human adaptation, indigenous knowledge, and socio-economic responses.

> Conservation management—how to foster habitat connectivity, sustainable agriculture, human-wildlife conflict mitigation, and other management practices.

The range of tasks for these projects is enormous and includes:

> Archeological work (e.g., digging trenches; sieving for artifacts and fossils; washing, sorting, recording, and packing findings).

> Participating in wildlife surveys (e.g., counting, tracking, or photographing birds, insects, fish, or animals).

> Feeding and caring for captive animals.

> Interviewing farmers or other locals.

> Educating locals about conservation.

> Gathering information about the environment (e.g., recording the structure and composition of forests, collecting water samples, sampling and measuring glacial sediments).

Earthwatch teams work in wildlife preserves, important historical sites, and national parks.

COST
At time of publication, programs cost from $500 to $4,600, excluding travel to and from the expedition site.

Included in the fee are in-country travel and lodging, meals, emergency medical and evacuation insurance for trips outside the U.S., and all field research costs (field permits, equipment, etc.). Neither airfare and costs incurred during free-time activities, nor visas and medical and trip cancellation insurance are included. Discounts are available for groups of six or more. Volunteers can fundraise their fees by opening an "Expedition Fund," into which tax deductible donations can be made. Please consult your tax advisor.

ACCOMMODATIONS
Accommodations vary by site and range from condos to hammocks to college dorm rooms. Meals also vary, from sumptuous buffets to cheese, crackers, and raisins that travel with you in your backpack.

FREE TIME
Generally, one or two days are built into each trip for local sightseeing. The researcher in charge can recommend local sights and attractions. In addition, many people choose to travel elsewhere in the country either before or after the project.

ORIENTATION
Upon signing up for a trip, volunteers receive an Expedition Briefing packet, including a packing list. Your researcher or one of the field staff will meet you at a designated in-country rendezvous point and conduct an on-site orientation.

APPLICATION PROCESS
Applications are accepted by phone or online on a first-come, first-serve basis until a team is full.

ADDITIONAL
Financial assistance, in the form of competitive grants,

is available for teachers and high school students (16+) applying for expeditions.

Earthwatch volunteer stories can be found on pages 85, 87, and 99 (Muriel Horacek, Schuyler Richardson, and the Petersons).

Global Citizens Network
130 N. Howell Street
St. Paul, MN 55104
Tel: 800-644-9292
Fax: 651-644-0960

info@globalcitizens.org
http://www.globalcitizens.org

ABOUT
Global Citizens Network sends teams of volunteers to communities where individuals immerse themselves for a short period of time in the local culture and daily life while partnering with a local grassroots organization, working to meet local needs. The teams generally consist of six to ten volunteers plus a trained team leader.

GCN seeks "to create a network of people who are committed to the shared values of peace, justice, tolerance, cross-cultural understanding, and global cooperation; to the preservation of indigenous cultures, traditions, and ecologies; and to the enhancement of the quality of life around the world." In describing its mission, GCN notes, "By providing participants the opportunity to learn about the society, knowledge, art, and livelihood of other cultures, Global Citizens Network seeks to honor and help preserve those cultures. By providing the resources of participating volunteers and project grants, Global Citizens Network seeks to assist human and community development in those cultures. By creating a network of people and organizations, Global Citizens Network also seeks to enhance participants' impact on issues of local and global concern."

GCN is a nonprofit organization with a staff of two full-time employees and one part-time assistant. It is guided by a volunteer board of directors comprised of people who have extensive experience in international travel, development, and cross-cultural education.

TIME REQUIREMENT

One to three weeks (including travel time), depending upon the site. Each day consists of both working and learning. GCN emphasizes that the work is actually only one part of the experience.

FOREIGN LANGUAGE REQUIREMENT

None; team leaders serve as translators when necessary. However, GCN asks that volunteers try and learn some basic phrases in order to enhance their experiences.

EXPERIENCE OR SKILLS NEEDED

No special skills or experience are required, but GCN looks for volunteers who are "culturally sensitive, flexible, optimistic, willing to both share and learn, work well in a team setting, and above all, are open to new experiences."

AGES

The minimum age is eighteen years when unaccompanied by a parent or guardian. Children as young as eight are permitted to accompany their parents or guardians. GCN welcomes families and asks that you consult with GCN staff before signing up for a trip with children under the age of twelve. GCN also will work with volunteers to plan a group trip. Family and youth discounts are available.

COUNTRIES

Brazil, Canada, Ecuador, Guatemala, Kenya, Mexico, Nepal, Peru, Tanzania, Thailand, U.S. (Arizona, Kentucky, Washington).

ACTIVITIES

Projects, which are determined and directed by partner communities, may not be decided upon until shortly before the arrival of a GCN team, and are subject to change. Past projects have been in three major areas:

- ▸ Community infrastructure construction—building a health clinic, renovating a youth center, improving a water drainage system, or installing playground equipment.
- ▸ Ecological/gardening—such as planting trees.
- ▸ Teaching in a primary school and installing playground equipment.

COST

At time of publication, programs cost $800-$2,200. Included in the fee are in-country travel and lodging, most meals, orientation materials, emergency medical and evacuation insurance for trips outside the U.S., donation to the village project, T-shirt, and a portion of GCN's program costs. Airfare, costs incurred during free-time activities, visas, and medical and trip cancellation insurance are not included. Fees also include part of the expenses of the trained team leader. Discounts are available for groups: in groups of four, one person travels half price; in groups of eight, one person travels free. Most trip-related expenses are tax-deductible for U.S. taxpayers. Please contact your tax advisor. Volunteers can fundraise their fees. Please note that tax law stipulates that any funds designated for a specific individual's volunteer program are NOT tax-deductible to the donor.

ACCOMMODATIONS

Accommodations vary by site. Home stays with local families are arranged whenever possible, but community centers and hotels are also used. At least one meal each day will be communal, with the team and community members eating together. Other meals are prepared either by team members or by a local cook.

FREE TIME

Generally two or three days are built into each trip for volunteers to explore and visit other places in the region at the volunteers' expense.

ORIENTATION

Upon signing up for a trip, volunteers receive an orientation manual with information on the country or state and the village, along with a reading list, packing list, and other health and travel tips. On-site orientation occurs on the first or second day of the trip.

APPLICATION PROCESS

Applications are accepted on a first-come, first-served basis until a team is full.

ADDITIONAL

GCN advises that college credit may be available for the experience and encourages college students to speak with their advisors.

School teachers may be able to earn 10 continuing education unit hours per week by participating in a GCN trip. Pre-approval by a local continuing education committee is required.

GCN volunteer stories can be found on pages 61, 64, 70, and 78 (David Taylor, Barb Everhart, and Anna Hadley).

Global Crossroad

415 East Airport Fwy.
Suite 365
Irving, TX 75062
Tel: 972-252-4191 (9am - 5pm)
Tel: 225-614-4695 (Off Office Hour)
Tel: 800-413-2008 (Within USA, Canada)
Fax: 972-636-1368, 972-636-1055

www.globalcrossroad.com
info@globalcrossroad.com

ABOUT

Global Crossroad is an international volunteer organization, offering a variety of placements to meet the needs of different volunteers, including individualized placements. Founded in 2003, Global Crossroad placed 1,800 volunteers in twenty-two countries in 2006. Global Crossroad's in-country coordinators work with established volunteer associations, including nonprofits and schools, to develop the projects for the volunteers and screen potential host families. Global Crossroad focuses on grassroots projects, cultural immersion, and travel learning.

Global Crossroad offers seven different types of programs. In addition to its "Volunteer Abroad" "Mini-Ventures," and "Summer Escape" programs, which are discussed here, it offers internships, paid teaching opportunities, humanitarian trips, scientific research expeditions, and Teaching English as a Foreign Language certification (TEFL).

TIME REQUIREMENT

Mini-Ventures are two weeks long, with several days spent volunteering. Summer Escapes last four weeks and include three weeks of volunteering and one week of country-wide travel. Volunteer Abroad projects range from two to twelve weeks, with the average project lasting six weeks. Volunteers work approximately twenty to thirty-five hours each week in these projects, with the remaining time devoted to cultural immersion and travel.

FOREIGN LANGUAGE REQUIREMENT
None. Global Crossroad provides one-to-two weeks of in-country language and cultural orientation for the Volunteer Abroad program.

EXPERIENCE OR SKILLS NEEDED
None.

AGES
For most countries, the minimum age is eighteen but for some of the Summer Escapes and a few of the deemed "safer countries," Global Crossroad does accept volunteers as young as sixteen years of age. For more information on age restrictions, please contact Global Crossroad.

COUNTRIES
Mini-Ventures: Costa Rica, Ecuador, Ghana, Honduras, India (Delhi and South), Kenya, Nepal, Peru, Sri Lanka, Tanzania, Thailand, Tibet.

Summer Escapes: China, Costa Rica, Ghana, Honduras, India, Kenya, Nepal, Peru, Tanzania Thailand, Tibet.

Volunteer Abroad: Argentina, Australia, Bolivia, Brazil, Cambodia, China, Costa Rica, Ecuador, Ghana, Guatemala, Honduras, India, Kenya, Mexico, Morocco, Namibia, Nepal, Peru, Philippines, Sri Lanka, South Africa, Tanzania, Thailand, Tibet, Togo, Uganda, Vietnam.

ACTIVITIES
Mini-Ventures, which include several days of volunteering within a two-week trip, focus on orphanages, but if

participants wish to volunteer in a project other than the orphanage, they may do so (please contact Global Crossroad for project availability).

Summer Escapes offer opportunities in local village service projects.

The "Volunteer Abroad" programs focus on:

▸ Infant and childcare—helping feed, clothe, and care for children in orphanages and children's homes.

▸ Supporting grassroots projects that assist and offer hope to the poor in rural areas, particularly women and children.

▸ Wildlife conservation—support ongoing wildlife research and preservation efforts while working alongside the conservationists, zoologists, wildlife researchers, and park managers.

▸ Eco-tourism and conservation.

COST

Fees vary by country and length of program. At the time of publication, they start at $799 for a four-week Summer Escape in China and range up to $3,000 for twelve-week volunteer programs in many countries. Fees include accommodations, meals, in-country transportation, emergency support (via two or three mobile telephone numbers), insurance coverage (travel health, travel accident insurance, travel assistance, travel language, and third-party liability), and the services and support of the in-country coordinator. Global Crossroad advises that program fees are NOT 100 percent tax-deductible for U.S. residents but that many people successfully fundraise their fees with fundraising material supplied by Global Crossroad. Please note that tax law stipulates that any funds designated for a specific individual's volunteer program are not tax-deductible to the donor. Please consult your tax advisor.

Airfare is not included.

ACCOMMODATIONS

Depending upon the volunteers' particular country, location, and situation, volunteers will either stay with a host family or in a rented house, hostel, or cabin. Volunteers stay in a single or shared room (with one other volunteer, depending on the host situation). Volunteers need to bring their own sleeping bags and other accessories.

FREE TIME

All of the Global Crossroad programs include extensive time for travel throughout the country, most often with a guide or the in-country coordinator. Volunteers have their weekends and evenings to themselves.

ORIENTATION

Prior to placement, Global Crossroad provides information about the country, including information about health, safety, and potential cultural shocks, and life with the host family. Depending on the country, each Volunteer Abroad volunteer spends the first one to two weeks in an orientation program, being immersed in the local language, joining cultural activities, taking city tours, and experiencing daily local life. The local in-country coordinator serves as support throughout the stay in the country.

APPLICATION PROCESS

Applicants may apply online via Global Crossroad's website: http://www.globalcrossroad.com/apply.php. If requiring an expedited placement, interested individuals are encouraged to contact Global Crossroad's offices.

ADDITIONAL

Global Crossroad partners with a United States-based university and offers college credit for its volunteer, intern, and teaching programs. Approved participants can earn up to fifteen quarter-hour credits (five quarter hours = 3.3 semester credits) depending on the duration of the projects.

Global Crossroad volunteer stories can be found on pages 83, 101, 104, and 120 (Janet McKelvey, Adam Forbes, John Donegan, and Chris Hanna).

Global Service Corps

300 Broadway
Suite 28
San Francisco, CA 94133-3312
Tel: 415-788-3666 x128
Fax: 415-788-7324

www.globalservicecorps.org
gsc@globalservicecorps.org

About

Global Service Corps (GSC) is a nonprofit international volunteer organization that creates opportunities for adult participants to live in developing nations and work on projects that serve Earth's people and her environment. These projects emphasize grassroots collaboration on the local level, promote mutual transfer of skills, and foster cross-cultural understanding. Its goals are to provide developing communities with the means to function more sustainably and to widen the perspectives of participants as responsible global citizens by revealing the challenges of life in developing nations.

GSC provides service-learning programs for people worldwide to live and work abroad in Thailand and Tanzania. Its view is that "the personal lives and activities of people around the world are increasingly intertwined. It is important that we understand the interrelatedness of our actions and the effect they have on individual health, social well-being, and environmental stability worldwide.

We are all responsible for the health of the whole world." It offers "a true cultural immersion," providing ways for volunteers to understand other cultures while actively addressing global issues at a community level. Group sizes vary depending upon the time of year; the summer months are the most popular and teams at that time average twelve participants.

Founded in 1994, GSC has become an established part of each community it serves. It started with a village-based program in Kenya, teaching bio-intensive agriculture to community members. GSC moved its East Africa Program to Tanzania in 2001. GSC has a staff of fifteen in the U.S. and in-country staff in both Tanzania and Thailand.

Global Service Corps is a recognized Non-Governmental Organization (NGO) in both Thailand and Tanzania. It has received official NGO status from the governments of Kenya, Tanzania, and Thailand.

TIME REQUIREMENT
Two-, four-, or six-week short-term programs, as well as internships and long-term programs that last from nine weeks to six months.

FOREIGN LANGUAGE REQUIREMENT
None.

EXPERIENCE OR SKILLS NEEDED
None.

AGES
Minimum age of eighteen for Thailand and twenty for Tanzania. In Thailand, children participating with their family are welcome, with discounted program fees for children: 75% for children ages sixteen to seventeen; 50% for children aged fifteen, and no fee for children fifteen or younger. Minimum age of twenty for Tanzania.

COUNTRIES

GSC provides services in two countries: Tanzania and Thailand.

ACTIVITIES

GSC offers six volunteer programs:

▸ English instruction (Thailand)—helping students and hospital staff improve their conversational English skills.

▸ Healthcare (Thailand)—shadowing Thai doctors and nurses while observing examinations, surgeries, and other hospital procedures.

▸ Sustainable agriculture (Tanzania and Thailand) —providing bio-intensive agriculture gardening seminars.

▸ HIV/AIDS prevention (Tanzania)—providing HIV/ AIDS awareness talks and seminars at local schools and community meetings. In the summer, Tanzania HIV/AIDS Prevention and Care participants can help lead the HIV/AIDS Life Skills Day Camp, training high school students to become peer health educators (three-week program plus one week of orientation and training).

▸ Buddhist Immersion Program (Thailand)—providing English language training at temple schools to novice monks and local school children while living on temple grounds or with local host families.

▸ Orphanage Program (Thailand)—Providing English training, mentorship, and companionship to young Thai orphans.

COST

At the time of publication, programs cost $2,315-2,815. Included in the fee are subsidized airport pickup, project transportation, accommodations, all meals, language and cultural training, weekend excursion, and project administration. The fees also support the in-country coordinators and other staff in Tanzania and Thailand. Participant fees and international airfare can be claimed as a tax deduction for U.S. taxpayers to the full extent of the law. Please consult your tax advisor. Discounts are available for family and friends: if a participant refers a friend or family member, he or she will receive a discount of 10 percent of the second participant's fees. Group rates also available.

ACCOMMODATIONS
Volunteers live with local families. Select programs in Thailand provide the option for private accommodations or accommodations in staff housing.

FREE TIME
All programs include one weekend excursion arranged by GSC. Participants have weekends free to travel or spend time with host families.

ORIENTATION
Global Service Corps provides one- or two-week training sessions at the start of each volunteer and internship program. In Thailand, this includes a two-day tour of Bangkok and a three-day cultural orientation, including Thai language training; an introduction to the specific project; a day trip to Wat San Phra Kan (Monkey Temple), in Lopburi, and Wat Phra Baht Nam Phu AIDS Hospice; and an overnight Buddhist immersion at a local Wat (Buddhist temple). GSC also provides basic training in TEFL (Teaching English as a Foreign Language). In Tanzania, orientation includes a discussion on cultural, health, and safety issues specific to the day-to-day realities of Tanzania;

Swahili language lessons; as well as an introduction to projects. The HIV Prevention Program includes training on HIV/AIDS Prevention and Care. The Sustainable Agriculture Program provides training on HIV/AIDS issues, in addition to nutrition and bio-intensive agriculture.

APPLICATION PROCESS
The initial application process includes submission of a refundable deposit, current resume, personal statement, and Participant Background Information form as supplied by GSC.

ADDITIONAL
GSC also offers long-term programs and internships, which require a minimum commitment of nine weeks. Premed and medical students, as well as healthcare professionals, can participate in the HIV/AIDS Prevention and Care or International Health internships. GSC also offers Seeds of Sustenance (SOS) Fellowship and Internship Programs for international development and public health professionals and graduate students.

The GSC volunteer story can be found on page 109 (Sara Spike).

Global Volunteers
375 E. Little Canada Road
St. Paul, MN 55117-1628
Tel: 800-487-1074
Fax: 651-482-0915

www.globalvolunteers.org

ABOUT
Global Volunteers, founded in 1984, is one of the original "volunteer vacation" organizations in the U.S. Mobilizing approximately 200 service-learning teams in

twenty countries each year, volunteers serve in partnership with local leaders and indigenous host organizations on human and economic development projects identified by the community as important to its long-term development. The volunteers live and work with local people to make a direct contribution to the on-going work project and thereby gain a firsthand understanding of how other people live. Direct work project funding and child sponsorships also support the host community year-around.

The Global Volunteers philosophy of service is "that to be successful in the effort to help others, outsiders must work at the invitation and under the direction of those they are attempting to assist." The organization also is dedicated to building a foundation for world peace by enabling people to make a contribution through service to others and increasing opportunities for mutual international understanding.

Since its inception twenty-four years ago, more than 21,000 people have participated in Global Volunteers programs. It has a worldwide staff of fifty-two and partners or collaborates with more than 200 organizations at the international, national, and local levels. Administrative offices are in the U.S., where Global Volunteers is a nonprofit 501(c)(3) organization. Country offices operate in approximately half of the host communities.

TIME REQUIREMENT
Two to three weeks. Each service program requires five full days of work each week. The service program begins on the day the team assembles in-country. Most volunteers traveling from the U.S. arrive one or two days before the service program begins.

LANGUAGE REQUIREMENT
None. Volunteers must be fluent in English.

Experience or Skills Needed

No prior experience or skills are required, although professional healthcare experience can influence medical assistance placement.

Ages

The minimum age is eighteen years to participate as an adult. However, most service programs have individual accommodations for minors traveling with a parent or guardian. Families are encouraged to volunteer together on several of the programs.

Countries

Australia, Brazil, China, Cook Islands, Costa Rica, Ecuador, Ghana, Greece, Hungary, India, Ireland, Italy, Jamaica, Mexico, Peru, Poland, Portugal, Romania, Tanzania, USA. Plans are to add a new partnership in South Africa in 2008.

Activities

Global Volunteer programs fall into five major areas:

▸ Teaching conversational English—primarily in classrooms but also at government agencies, as well as intensive English language summer camps. Sometimes instruction in other subjects, such as the sciences, computer literacy, and mathematics, is included.

▸ Childcare—providing extra sets of hands to help care for and offer attention, nurturing, and love to vulnerable and at-risk children in failure-to-thrive clinics, orphanages, and children's homes.

▸ Community infrastructure and general labor—typical projects include assisting with building tables, chairs, and desks for schools; erecting community centers and playgrounds, and painting and landscaping.

▸ Providing healthcare—Healthcare professionals help treat people in need, providing patient examinations, dental and eye examinations, prenatal care, vaccinations, and general public health education.

Volunteer programs are conducted in orphanages, childcare centers, schools, health clinics and hospitals, homes for the elderly, centers for people with disabilities, and other community organizations, primarily in rural locations.

COST

At the time of publication, the service program fee for one-, two- or three-week international service programs ranges from $1,370 to $2,750. Some discounts—totaling up to $800—are available. All expenses, including airfare, are tax-deductible for U.S. taxpayers. The organization's Canadian status is pending and will provide tax deductibility for Canadians in 2008. Volunteers can fundraise their fees. Global Volunteers provides an online guide for fundraising. Please note that tax law stipulates that any funds designated for a specific individual's volunteer program are NOT tax-deductible to the donor. Please consult your tax advisor.

The service program fee includes direct work project funding provided to the host community, and also covers the volunteer's on-site expenses, including food, lodging (generally double occupancy), ground transportation in the host community, project materials, orientation materials, and individual emergency evacuation insurance. The fee also covers the expenses of the trained team leader.

Airfare or other travel to the host community is not included. Visas, free-time expenses, alcoholic beverages, and medical and trip cancellation insurance expenses are also the volunteer's responsibility.

ACCOMMODATIONS

Volunteers usually stay at tourist-class hotels in the community where they work; occasionally guest houses are used in remote rural communities. The entire team stays in the same facility, most often has morning and evening meals together, and meets each evening. Depending upon the location, meals are either taken at local restaurants or prepared for the group by a local inhabitant; the food is typical for the country and region. Many times, community members eat the afternoon meal with the volunteers to provide an opportunity for conversation.

FREE TIME

Free time is available most evenings and every weekend. The local staff can provide a list of activities previous teams have explored and enjoyed. Most volunteers wait until they are with the team to plan activities with their team members.

ORIENTATION

In-country orientation is run by the team leader with local support. It can include team-building sessions, an in-depth orientation to the host community, guest speakers (e.g., traditional healers or community activists), and such educational events as musical concerts and round-table discussions.

APPLICATION PROCESS

A discount is provided for applying online at the Global Volunteers website. Trained volunteer coordinators are available by phone or e-mail to help prospective volunteers select a service program that suits their abilities and interests.

Global Volunteers volunteer stories can be found on pages 57, 63, 112, 115, 124, 130, and 133 (Coretta Bedsole, the Petersons, and Gloria Gery).

Hands On New Orleans
4153 Canal Street
New Orleans, LA 70119
Tel: 504-483-7041
Fax: 504-483-7043

www.handsonneworleans.org
volunteer@handsonneworleans.org

ABOUT
Points of Light & Hands On Network inspire and mobilize people to become engaged, take action, and solve community problems. The organization supports a network of 370 affiliates and eight international locations. Collectively, they mobilize millions of volunteers who partner with thousands of nonprofits, schools, and community organizations every year. By cultivating a dynamic network of linked civic hubs, corporate partners, nonprofits, and citizen leaders who engage volunteers in meaningful community change, they are building a change movement—achieving scale and impact by inspiring a culture of service and offering practical tools, new ideas, and innovation to the civic space. The mission of the organization is to "inspire and motivate people to meet critical community needs by encouraging active citizenship through meaningful service."

In operation since the devastating hurricane Katrina in 2005, Hands On New Orleans has been assisting cleaning and rebuilding much of the city. It has engaged over 5,000 volunteers, producing over 400,000 hours of service, which have resulted in over 400 housing repair projects, rebuilding of one major music venue, building one library, and assisting 27 Kaboom! Playground builds. Its vision is a "greater New Orleans as a hub of civic-minded individuals that take action through service to meet critical community needs."

TIME REQUIREMENT
One day, up to three months.

LANGUAGE REQUIREMENT
None.

EXPERIENCE OR SKILLS NEEDED
No prior experience or skills are required for most projects.

AGES
Minimum age is eighteen.

COUNTRIES
Points of Light & the Hands On Network have affiliates in 370 areas in the U.S., as well as in Australia, Brazil, China, Japan, The Netherlands, The Philippines, South Korea, and Zimbabwe.

ACTIVITIES
Projects at Hands On New Orleans depend on immediate needs and include:

- House gutting—removing interiors of homes that suffered water damage during Katrina.
- Mold removal—trained by experienced mold remediation professionals and indoor air-quality specialists, volunteer teams clean entire houses of mold.
- Beautification projects—removing trash and debris left by Katrina.
- Food bank distribution—organizing donated food items, packing grocery bags for patrons, and assisting in distributing those bags.
- Animal shelter support—performing many of the tasks necessary for running animal shelters, includ-

ing landscaping, painting, cleaning the grounds and interior, and washing the animals.

‣ Wetlands restoration.

‣ Assisting local nonprofits—helping local institutions, including schools, shelters, and community centers.

Volunteers are asked to come to New Orleans with an open mind, understanding that available opportunities may not always match their skills and interests. As soon as a project is approved and funded that fits volunteers' skill sets or interests, they will be assigned to it.

COST

At the time of publication, volunteers arrange their own travel to New Orleans and are asked to provide a donation of $20/week, which covers three meals each day, transportation to and from project sites, Internet access, and the cost of tools and equipment for the projects.

ACCOMMODATIONS

Hands On New Orleans provides housing in which bathrooms, showers, and dining areas are shared. Sleeping quarters are dormitory style, segregated by sex. Volunteers maintain the facility by assisting in setting up breakfast, cooking evening dinners, and helping to keep the facility clean.

FREE TIME

Every evening, there is a community meeting, which allows for volunteers to share and report on their experience that day. This is also a time where volunteers find out about the following day's projects and are given the opportunity to select their project for that day. After that, evenings are free for socializing with other volunteers or sightseeing in New Orleans.

ORIENTATION

All volunteers are provided with orientation and training upon arrival.

APPLICATION PROCESS

Hands On New Orleans has a capacity of up to sixty volunteers at any one time, so volunteers should apply ahead of time. To apply, send an e-mail to volunteer@handsonneworleans.org or call 504-895-4238.

The Hands On New Orleans volunteer story can be found on page 82 (Helene and Alan Kahan).

i-to-i Meaningful Travel, North America

190 E. 9th Avenue, Suite 350
Denver, CO 80203
Tel: 303-991-5407
www.i-to-i.com

ABOUT

i-to-i Meaningful Travel, part of the international i-to-i, is a volunteer travel provider that coordinates international volunteer vacations, as well as trains people to teach English as a foreign language (TEFL); the organization arranges volunteer and paid teaching placements abroad. In addition, i-to-i offers "meaningful tours," group tours that include cultural immersion activities and opportunities to teach English. Founded in 1994, i-to-i has sent approximately 20,000 volunteers to work on projects in overseas communities. It maintains offices in the United Kingdom, Ireland, and Australia, as well as the United States, and has a worldwide staff of 130. In-country support teams are available in every country with volunteer projects.

Founder Deirdre Bounds says, "I'm a firm believer that commerce and ethics can mix, which is why i-to-i is a commercial enterprise. My motivation was that a well-run business could help change the world with a focus on customer service, firm goals, and determined people."

TIME REQUIREMENT
One to twenty-four weeks; multiple projects can be combined.

LANGUAGE REQUIREMENT
None.

EXPERIENCE OR SKILLS NEEDED
No prior experience or skills are required for most projects, although healthcare volunteering can draw on professional healthcare experience, and media volunteering may require communications/journalism education or experience.

AGES
Minimum age is eighteen years for most programs. i-to-i has an "early Gap" program for sixteen- to nineteen-year-olds. Two-week volunteer programs are offered each summer in a variety of countries. In addition, children under sixteen can go on a number of volunteer vacations with their families. i-to-i Meaningful Travel works with families on a case-by-case basis to make appropriate placements.

COUNTRIES
Argentina, Australia, Bolivia, Brazil, Cambodia, China, Costa Rica, Dominica, Dominican Republic, Ecuador, Egypt ("meaningful tours" only), Ghana, Honduras, India, Indonesia, Kenya, Laos, Madagascar, Malaysia, Mexico, Morocco ("meaningful tours" only), Nepal, New Zealand, Panama, Peru, Philippines, South Africa, Sri Lanka, Tanzania, Thailand, Tibet ("meaningful tours" only), Trinidad & Tobago, Uganda, Vietnam, Zambia.

ACTIVITIES

▸ Community service/community development—
  providing life skills for children in orphanages, shelters, and schools, or working with adults in residential homes; these also include teaching English
  as a foreign language (TEFL).
▸ Conservation/historical preservation—including
  planting, maintenance activities at parks, collecting stray animals, and helping with education and
  awareness campaigns.
▸ Construction—helping to build homes and schools.
▸ Healthcare—assisting hospital staff, providing information to patients and parents, taking care of
  and playing with young patients; for those with
  appropriate knowledge and experience, training
  hospital staff.
▸ Media—English writing and editing for a variety of
  media, arts administration, and film production.
▸ Athletics—coaching at schools, orphanages, and
  community centers.
▸ Teaching—English; general education from kinder-
  garten to university level; and special programs
  including music, special needs children, business
  and technology schools, orphanages, and community cooperatives. (When volunteering for teaching, i-to-i provides complimentary teacher training.)

COST
At the time of publication, the fees start at $800. The
fees include trip planning and pre-departure advice, lodging, meals with many (but not all) projects, ground transportation, in-country orientation, and 24 hr/7 days per
week support network.
Airfare is not included.

ACCOMMODATIONS
Varies, from the home of a local family to a hotel or

guesthouse. Some projects include group lodging in a volunteer house.

FREE TIME
Free time is available some afternoons, evenings, and weekends. The in-country support team can advise on where best to go. After their volunteer projects, some i-to-i volunteers travel with other volunteers they met on the trip.

ORIENTATION
In-country orientation is run by the in-country staff.

APPLICATION PROCESS
The minimum booking deadline is two weeks, and i-to-i recommends six months or more on particularly popular projects. Some conservation and media projects are filled a year in advance. A $275 deposit is required.

i-to-i volunteer stories can be found on pages 90, 94, 97, and 130 (Stephanie Kwong, Jane Stanfield, and Kelly Ferguson).

International Senior Lawyers Project
31 W. 52nd Street, 9th Floor
New York, NY 10019
Tel: 212-895-1022

www.islp.org
information@islp.org

ABOUT
The International Senior Lawyers Project (ISLP) provides volunteer legal services by skilled and experienced attorneys to help institute and implement legal reforms, advance the social and economic well-being of people in developing countries, and build the capacity of local

organizations and professionals to meet the needs of their communities.

ISLP was incorporated in March 2000 and is a non-profit, 501(c)3 organization. Its founders—a group of public-spirited senior partners of global law firms—believe that there is a widespread need throughout the developing world for legal assistance from experienced attorneys and a growing pool of attorneys at or near retirement age who have both the ability to help meet that demand and the desire to serve the world community.

TIME REQUIREMENT
One week to over one year, plus preparatory time before travel. Most projects require a one- to six-month commitment.

LANGUAGE REQUIREMENT
None.

EXPERIENCE OR SKILLS NEEDED
Volunteers must be practicing or retired attorneys.

AGES
Minimum age is twenty-five years, although most volunteers are at a senior level, with many retired from active practice.

COUNTRIES
ISLP works in Southeast Asia, Africa, Eastern Europe, and Russia. Projects in recent years have been based in Bosnia, Bulgaria, the Czech Republic, Ethiopia, Hungary, India, Liberia, Lithuania, Mongolia, Nigeria, Romania, Russia, Rwanda, South Africa, Tanzania, Uganda, and Ukraine.

ACTIVITIES
ISLP focuses on three program areas:

▸ Human rights and social welfare—experienced lawyers work on-site with foreign non-governmental organizations (NGOs) such a Liberian women's advocacy organization and a Mongolian organization seeking to build its environmental advocacy program.

▸ Economic development and participation in the global economy—providing teaching and training programs for business lawyers and government officials, legal assistance to social entrepreneurs, assisting microloan and venture capital funds, and promoting law reform that encourages economic development.

▸ Access to justice—supplying assistance to burgeoning public defender offices and promoting the development of organized pro bono programs, such as the first public defenders offices in Ukraine.

Within these program areas, ISLP provides three kinds of services:

▸ On-site volunteers to help strengthen and build the capacity of local non-governmental organizations (NGOs), government agencies, and other institutions.

▸ Expert legal counsel on corporate, transactional, litigation, and legislative matters.

▸ Cross-border research and analysis on human rights and other issues.

COST
The costs involved with each project vary widely.

ACCOMMODATIONS
The local NGO partner assists volunteers in locating private accommodations in each country.

FREE TIME

Work follows the work week of the host country, providing ample free time on weekends.

ORIENTATION

ISLP provides support to volunteers before, during, and after assignments through country and project briefings, a Memo of Understanding outlining project goals, and final reports from volunteers and the NGO partners.

APPLICATION PROCESS

ISLP has an online application that requests, among other details, current or past legal expertise, language and training skills, and period of time available for a project. Volunteers also can specify how much notice they require before leaving for a project, from one month to six months or longer.

The ISLP volunteer story can be found on page 21 (Susan Colman).

COUNTRY-ORGANIZATION MATCH

Listed below are the organizations included in this book by the country each organization serves. Many of these organizations partner with nonprofit organizations in various countries so the list that they work in is constantly changing as certain projects are completed or others are added. If your first and second choice organizations don't appear to serve your first and second choice country, be sure and check with the organizations to see if those countries have been added.

Arctic	Earthwatch
Argentina	Earthwatch, Global Crossroad, i-to-i Meaningful Travel
Australia	Earthwatch, Global Crossroad, Global Volunteers, i-to-i Meaningful Travel
Bahamas	Earthwatch
Belarus	Earthwatch
Belize	Earthwatch
Bohemia	Earthwatch
Bolivia	Global Crossroad, i-to-i Meaningful Travel

Bosnia	The International Senior Lawyers Project
Botswana	Earthwatch
Brazil	Cross-Cultural Solutions, Earthwatch, Global Citizens Network, Global Crossroad, Global Volunteers, i-to-i Meaningful Travel
Bulgaria	The International Senior Lawyers Project
Cambodia	AJWS, Global Crossroad, i-to-i Meaningful Travel
Cameroon	Earthwatch
Canada	Earthwatch, Global Citizens Network
China	Cross-Cultural Solutions, Earthwatch, Global Crossroad, Global Volunteers, i-to-i Meaningful Travel
Cook Islands	Global Volunteers
Costa Rica	Cross-Cultural Solutions, Earthwatch, Global Crossroad, Global Volunteers, i-to-i Meaningful Travel
Czech Republic	The International Senior Lawyers Project
Dominica	i-to-i Meaningful Travel
Dominican Republic	AJWS, i-to-i Meaningful Travel
Easter Islands	Earthwatch
Ecuador	Earthwatch, Global Citizens Network, Global Crossroad, Global Volunteers, i-to-i Meaningful Travel
Egypt	i-to-i Meaningful Travel
El Salvador	AJWS
England	Earthwatch
Ethiopia	The International Senior Lawyers Project
Ghana	AJWS, Cross-Cultural Solutions, Global Crossroad, Global Volunteers, i-to-i Meaningful Travel

Greece	Earthwatch, Global Volunteers
Guatemala	AJWS, Cross-Cultural Solutions, Global Citizens Network, Global Crossroad
Honduras	AJWS, Global Crossroad, i-to-i Meaningful Travel
Hungary	Global Volunteers, The International Senior Lawyers Project
Iceland	Earthwatch
India	AJWS, Cross-Cultural Solutions, Global Crossroad, Global Volunteers, i-to-i Meaningful Travel, The International Senior Lawyers Project
Indonesia	i-to-i Meaningful Travel
Ireland	Global Volunteers
Italy	Global Volunteers
Jamaica	Global Volunteers
Japan	Earthwatch
Kenya	Earthwatch, Global Citizens Network, Global Crossroad, i-to-i Meaningful Travel
Laos	i-to-i Meaningful Travel
Liberia	The International Senior Lawyers Project
Lithuania	The International Senior Lawyers Project
Madagascar	Earthwatch, i-to-i Meaningful Travel
Malaysia	Earthwatch, i-to-i Meaningful Travel
Mexico	AJWS, Earthwatch, Global Citizens Network, Global Crossroad, Global Volunteers, i-to-i Meaningful Travel
Mongolia	The International Senior Lawyers Project
Morocco	Cross-Cultural Solutions, Global Crossroad, i-to-i Meaningful Travel
Namibia	Earthwatch, Global Crossroad

Nepal	Global Citizens Network, Global Crossroad, i-to-i Meaningful Travel
New Zealand	Earthwatch, i-to-i Meaningful Travel
Nicaragua	AJWS
Nigeria	The International Senior Lawyers Project
Panama	i-to-i Meaningful Travel
Peru	AJWS, Cross-Cultural Solutions, Earthwatch, Global Citizens Network, Global Crossroad, Global Volunteers, i-to-i Meaningful Travel
Philippines	Global Crossroad, i-to-i Meaningful Travel
Poland	Global Volunteers
Portugal	Earthwatch, Global Volunteers
Puerto Rico	Earthwatch
Romania	Earthwatch, Global Volunteers, The International Senior Lawyers Project
Russia	Cross-Cultural Solutions, Earthwatch, The International Senior Lawyers Project
Rwanda	The International Senior Lawyers Project
Senegal	AJWS
Seychelles	Earthwatch
South Africa	AJWS, Cross-Cultural Solutions, Earthwatch, Global Crossroad, Global Volunteers, i-to-i Meaningful Travel, The International Senior Lawyers Project
Spain	Earthwatch
Sri Lanka	Earthwatch, Global Crossroad, Global Crossroad, i-to-i Meaningful Travel
Tanzania	Cross-Cultural Solutions, Global Citizens Network, Global Crossroad,

	Global Service Corps, Global Volunteers, i-to-i Meaningful Travel
Thailand	AJWS, Cross-Cultural Solutions, Educational Network for Grassroots and Global Exchange, Earthwatch, Global Citizens Network, Global Crossroad, Global Service Corps, i-to-i Meaningful Travel
Tibet	Global Crossroad, i-to-i Meaningful Travel
Togo	Global Crossroad
Trinidad & Tobago	i-to-i Meaningful Travel
Uganda	AJWS, Global Crossroad, i-to-i Meaningful Travel, The International Senior Lawyers Project
Ukraine	The International Senior Lawyers Project
United States	Earthwatch, Global Citizens Network, Global Volunteers, Hands On New Orleans
Vietnam	Earthwatch, Global Crossroad
Vietnam	i-to-i Meaningful Travel
Zambia	i-to-i Meaningful Travel

Animal conservation in South Africa.

GUIDE TO COUNTRIES FEATURED
IN THIS BOOK

COUNTRY	VOLUNTEER	CHAPTER
Australia	Jane Stanfield	Chapter 8
Australia	Muriel Horacek	Chapter 8
China	Petersons	Chapter 11
Cook Islands	Petersons	Chapter 9
Costa Rica	Schuyler Richardson	Chapter 4
Costa Rica	Petersons	Chapter 5
Costa Rica	Muriel Horacek	Chapter 8
Costa Rica	Stephanie Kwong	Chapter 8
Ecuador	Petersons	Chapter 10
Ghana	John Donegan	Chapter 9
Honduras	Maya Brodkey	Chapter 5
Ireland	Coretta Bedsole	Chapter 5
Israel	Suzanne Stone	Chapter 6
Israel	Suzanne Stone	Chapter 2
Kenya	Chris Hanna	Chapter 10
Kenya	Kelly Ferguson	Chapter 11
Mexico	Petersons	Chapter 11
Mexico	Barb Everhart	Chapter 5
Nepal	Adam Forbes	Chapter 8

Romania	Gloria Gery	Chapter 10
Russia	Corey Stilts	Chapter 10
Russia	Sarah Forman	Chapter 10
Senegal	Laura Silver	Chapter 4
South Africa	Jane Stanfield	Chapter 8
Sri Lanka	Janet McKelvey	Chapter 7
Tanzania	David Taylor	Chapter 5
Tanzania	Sara Spike	Chapter 9
Thailand	Liz O' Callahan	Chapter 2
Thailand	Anna Hadley	Chapter 5
Uganda	Susan Colman	Chapter 2
United States (Hawaii)	Petersons	Chapter 8
United States (Idaho)	Schuyler Richardson	Chapter 8
United States (Louisiana)	Kahans	Chapter 7
United States (Minnesota)	Coretta Bedsole	Chapter 11
United States (Virginia)	Christa Lyons	Chapter 2
United States (Washington)	Barb Everhart	Chapter 6

PROJECT-ORGANIZATION MATCH

Listed below are the organizations included in this book by the type of volunteer activity also included in this book. I have combined many activities into broad categories. For example, "Healthcare" can include delivering healthcare, assisting hospital staff, and providing public health education, especially about HIV/AIDS.

Similarly, "Environmental Work and Conservation" is a very broad topic, encompassing sustainable agriculture projects, other planting and gardening activities, wildlife surveys and tracking, feeding and caring for animals, and gathering information about the environment.

Teaching can include teaching English as a second language, coaching athletics, and teaching any academic subject at almost any educational level from pre-school through university, and teaching in art and music programs.

BUSINESS DEVELOPMENT:
AJWS, Educational Network for Grassroots and Global Exchange, Global Crossroad, Hands On New Orleans, i-to-i Meaningful Travel, The International Senior Lawyers Project.

CONSTRUCTION:
Global Citizens Network, Global Volunteers, Hands On New Orleans, i-to-i Meaningful Travel

CULTURAL PRESERVATION:
Earthwatch, Global Citizens Network, i-to-i Meaningful Travel

DISASTER RELIEF:
Global Crossroad, Hands On New Orleans

ENVIRONMENTAL WORK AND CONSERVATION:
AJWS, Earthwatch, Educational Network for Grassroots and Global Exchange, Global Citizens Network, Global Crossroad, Global Service Corps, i-to-i Meaningful Travel

HEALTHCARE:
AJWS, Cross Cultural Solutions, Global Service Corps, Global Volunteers, i-to-i Meaningful Travel

SOCIAL SERVICES:
AJWS, Cross Cultural Solutions, Educational Network for Grassroots and Global Exchange, Global Crossroad, Global Service Corps, Global Volunteers, Hands On New Orleans, i-to-i Meaningful Travel

TEACHING:
AJWS, Cross Cultural Solutions, Global Citizens Network, Global Service Corps, Global Volunteers, i-to-i Meaningful Travel

ABOUT THE AUTHOR

Suzanne Stone has spent her professional life working for charities and other nonprofit organizations and volunteers in her spare time. Currently, vice president, finance & administration, for the Society for Women's Health Research, she is also a docent and Visitor Information Specialist at the Smithsonian Institution. She has traveled to a dozen countries. The inspiration for this book is her own volunteer vacation, which provided a different intercultural experience and a new view of a country she had visited many times.